What are Qualitative Research Ethics?

'What is?' Research Methods series

Edited by Graham Crow, University of Southampton

ISSN: 2048–6812

The 'What is?' series provides authoritative introductions to a range of research methods which are at the forefront of developments in the social sciences. Each volume sets out the key elements of the particular method and features examples of its application, drawing on a consistent structure across the whole series. Written in an accessible style by leading experts in the field, this series is an innovative pedagogical and research resource.

What is Online Research?
Using the Internet for Social Science Research
Tristram Hooley, Jane Wellens and John Marriott
ISBN (HB):   9781780933344
ISBN (PB):   9781849665247
ISBN (ebook): 9781849665551

What is Social Network Analysis?
John Scott
ISBN (HB):   9781780938486
ISBN (PB):   9781849668170
ISBN (ebook): 9781849668194

What is Qualitative Research?
Martyn Hammersley
ISBN (HB):   9781780933351
ISBN (PB):   9781849666060
ISBN (ebook): 9781849666091

What are Qualitative Research Ethics?
Rose Wiles
ISBN (HB):   9781780938509
ISBN (PB):   9781849666527
ISBN (ebook): 9781849666541

What is Discourse Analysis?
Stephanie Taylor
ISBN (HB):   9781780938493
ISBN (PB):   9781849669030
ISBN (ebook): 9781849669061

What are Community Studies?
Graham Crow
ISBN (HB):   9781780933337
ISBN (PB):   9781849665957
ISBN (ebook): 9781849665988

Forthcoming books:

What is Qualitative Interviewing?
Rosalind Edwards and Janet Holland
ISBN (HB):   9781780938523
ISBN (PB):   9781849668095
ISBN (ebook): 9781849668019

What is Narrative Research?
Molly Andrews, Mark Davis, Cigdem Esin, Lar-Christer Hyden, Margareta Hyden, Corinne Squire and Barbara Harrison
ISBN (HB):   9781849669702
ISBN (PB):   9781849669733
ISBN (ebook): 9781849669702

What is Inclusive Research?
Melanie Nind
ISBN (HB):   9781780938516
ISBN (PB):   9781849668118
ISBN (ebook): 9781849668125

What are
qualitative
research ethics?

Rose Wiles

B L O O M S B U R Y
LONDON • NEW DELHI • NEW YORK • SYDNEY

Bloomsbury Academic

An imprint of Bloomsbury Publishing Plc

50 Bedford Square   175 Fifth Avenue
London   New York
WC1B 3DP   NY 10010
UK   USA

www.bloomsbury.com

First published 2013

© Rose Wiles, 2013

CIP records for this book are available from the British Library
and the Library of Congress

ISBN: HB: 978-1-78093-850-9
        PB: 978-1-84966-652-7

Printed and bound in Great Britain by
MPG Books Group, Bodmin, Cornwall.

Contents

Series foreword

The idea behind this series is a simple one: to provide concise and accessible overviews of a range of frequently-used research methods and of current issues in research methodology. Books in the series have been written by experts in their fields with a brief to write about their subject for a broad audience who are assumed to be interested but not necessarily to have any prior knowledge. The series is a natural development of presentations made in the 'What is?' strand at Economic and Social Research Council Research Methods Festivals which have proved popular both at the Festivals themselves and subsequently as a resource on the website of the ESRC National Centre for Research Methods.

Methodological innovation is the order of the day, and the 'What is?' format allows researchers who are new to a field to gain an insight into its key features, while also providing a useful update on recent developments for people who have had some prior acquaintance with it. All readers should find it helpful to be taken through the discussion of key terms, the history of how the method or methodological issue has developed, and the assessment of the strengths and possible weaknesses of the approach through analysis of illustrative examples.

Research ethics has come to be one of the most contentious areas of contemporary social scientific research, and this book conveys the key issues of contention and how researchers in the field of qualitative research have responded to them. That it manages to do so in a measured and systematic fashion is no small feat. In addition, it provides an analysis of the ethical concerns that continue to arise with new developments in the field, suggesting that while these do present serious challenges to researchers, there are good reasons to believe that ethical ways of responding to them are being developed.

The books cannot provide information about their subject matter down to a fine level of detail, but they will equip readers with a powerful sense of reasons why it deserves to be taken seriously and, it is hoped, with the enthusiasm to put that knowledge into practice.

Graham Crow
Series editor

1 Introduction

This book provides an introduction to research ethics relevant to qualitative research across the social sciences. It outlines approaches for thinking about ethical issues in qualitative social research and the key ethical issues that need consideration. It is intended to have relevance for researchers and students working across a range of social science disciplines and it explores ethical issues relating to 'traditional' research approaches, such as ethnography, interviews and focus groups, as well as those relating to new and emerging methods and approaches, particularly visual and online methods.

There has been an increasing interest in research ethics in the twenty-first century in the light of the increasing ethical regulation of social research. Various authors working in qualitative social science, particularly ethnographers, have contested the appropriateness of ethical regulation in social research. These academics have argued that qualitative research poses minimal risks to participants and that ethical review of research by research ethics committees is both unnecessary and detrimental to social science research (Atkinson, 2009; Dingwall, 2008; Hammersley, 2009). An alternative and perhaps less popular view is that social science research is never risk free and that systems of ethical review encourage researchers to think through ethical issues and to develop their ethical thinking (Boulton *et al*, 2004). Despite considerable critiques of regulation, systems of ethical review have become embedded in most research institutions. This has heightened researchers' awareness of ethical issues and highlighted the need for training and resources to enhance researchers' 'ethical literacy'. Much of the drive for researchers in this area has been to enable them to manage the institutional ethical review process and a number of excellent resources have been developed with this aim in mind (for example http://www.ethicsguidebook.ac.uk/).

However, enhancing 'ethical literacy' means more than learning how to achieve ethics approval. 'Ethical literacy' means encouraging researchers to understand and engage with ethical issues as they emerge throughout the process of research and not merely to view research ethics as something that is completed once a favourable opinion on a proposed research project has been granted by a research ethics committee. While it may be the case that some ethical issues can be anticipated prior to a study commencing, often ethical issues emerge as research proceeds, sometimes in unexpected and surprising ways.

An argument frequently put forward by social researchers is that ethical decision making is inevitably situational and contextual and cannot be determined by appeal to predetermined codes and principles. It is argued that decisions about ethical issues that emerge in the process of research need to be decided on 'in the field' in the light of the specific issue, the people involved and the likely consequences. This is sometimes used as an argument against ethical regulation in general which is viewed as limiting researchers' ability to act on the situation that arises. It is also used as an argument against the use of ethical frameworks (particularly principlism) in ethical decision making. It is argued that a 'one size fits all' approach such as principlism, in which issues such as informed consent and anonymity are viewed as essential principles to be upheld in all social research, is limiting and prevents researchers making ethical decisions in the context of their research in the ways that meet the needs of their research participants.

It is a central theme of this book that consideration of ethical frameworks is important in helping to guide researchers in thinking through the ethical challenges with which they are confronted. This is not to argue that ethical dilemmas are anything other than situational and contextual; consideration of ethical frameworks does not preclude individual deliberation on the part of researchers. The ethical dilemmas that researchers encounter in research are essentially moral dilemmas. Researchers may have a 'gut feeling' about the morally 'right' course of action in a situation that they encounter. However, ethical frameworks can help them to think about, evaluate and justify these 'gut feelings'. Ethical frameworks do not provide clear answers to such dilemmas, simply a means of thinking about them and assessing what an appropriate and defensible course of action might be. Such actions might differ according to the ethical framework used and an individual researcher's moral views. The important issue is that researchers use a framework that fits with their moral views and which enables them to explore and justify the decisions they make.

The focus of this book is based on three premises: first, that researchers need to consider ethical issues throughout the entirety of their research; second, that gaining an understanding of the different philosophical approaches to research ethics and identifying an approach that fits with their moral and intellectual framework will help them to engage with issues that emerge as their research unfolds; and third, that, despite the well-known horror stories of unethical conduct, most ethical issues with which researchers grapple are relatively mundane and everyday, but no less important for that. The book focuses primarily on ethical issues that emerge for researchers and research participants in the conduct of research. Researchers also have ethical responsibilities to the research team with whom they may be working, to their discipline, to the wider research community and to the public. It is incumbent on researchers to consider ethical issues within this broader context.

The book commences with an exploration of ethical frameworks as well as various forms of guidelines and regulation that guide or inform ethical decision making. This chapter also outlines relevant legislation with which researchers are obliged to comply.

The following three chapters explore three of the core issues in research ethics and the ways that researchers have engaged with them: informed consent; anonymity and confidentiality; and risk. In each of these chapters the meaning of these concepts are explored and their application, and in some cases their relevance, in different types of research approaches is outlined. In each of these three chapters, examples are provided from the literature of the ways in which researchers have managed these ethical issues in their research. Examples are also drawn on from a research project on informed consent conducted with my colleagues Sue Heath, Graham Crow and Vikki Charles as part of the Economic and Social Research Council (ESRC) Research Methods Programme as well as a project on ethical issues in visual methods conducted with my colleagues Jon Prosser, Amanda Coffey, Sue Heath and Judy Robison. Each of these projects involved interviews or focus groups with researchers exploring their views about ethical issues in qualitative research and how these issues were managed in the context of their research.

Chapter six discusses common ethical dilemmas that researchers experience and through three detailed case studies discusses the deliberation and management of such dilemmas. Finally, chapter seven explores developments in research methods over the last decade and the ethical challenges that these raise. Developments in narrative, participatory, visual, digital and e-research methods and data-sharing are discussed and the extent to which these demand new approaches to research ethics or the re-working of familiar issues in new contexts. A list of resources where further information on the various issues discussed in the book can be found is provided.

There are a number of key terms used in the literature on ethics. These are explained throughout this book. A brief definition of the key terms is given here; further information on them can be found in the relevant chapters.

Key terms

Moral judgements/morality

Morality is concerned with intentions and actions which are good (or the 'right' thing to do) contrasted with those that are bad or wrong. A moral judgement is made when a person decides what the right course of action is in a specific situation. Ethical dilemmas in research involve people making moral judgements.

Ethics

Ethics is the branch of philosophy which addresses questions about morality. The terms ethics and morals are often used interchangeably. Research ethics are concerned with moral behaviour in research contexts.

Ethical frameworks

Ethical frameworks provide a means of thinking about ethical dilemmas (or moral behaviour). They provide some criteria against which researchers can consider what it is right or wrong to do when presented with an ethical dilemma. Common ethical frameworks are consequentialist, principlist, non-consequentialist, ethics of care and virtue ethics.

Consequentialist approaches

Consequentialist approaches argue that ethical decisions should be based on the consequences of specific actions so that an action is morally right if it will produce a good outcome for an individual or for wider society.

Principlist approaches

Principlist approaches are non-consequentialist approaches. Rather than focusing on the consequences of an action, they draw on the principles of respect for people's autonomy, beneficence, non-maleficence and justice in making and guiding ethical decisions in research. Respect for *autonomy* relates to issues of voluntariness, informed consent, confidentiality and anonymity. *Beneficence* concerns the responsibility to do good, *non-maleficence* concerns the responsibility to avoid harm and *justice* concerns the importance of the benefits and burdens of research being distributed equally. People using principlist approaches make ethical decisions on the basis of these specific principles. Principlist approaches hold that consent to participate in research should be freely given and that potential participants should not experience any form of coercion to encourage them to take part in research.

Ethics of care

An ethics of care approach means that ethical decisions are made on the basis of care, compassion and a desire to act in ways that benefit the individual or group who are the focus of research. This contrasts with consequentialist and principlist approaches which involve using rules or principles to address ethical dilemmas. An ethics of care approach means that researchers make decisions about ethical issues in relation to a particular case and by drawing on the notion of 'care' in relation to research participants, rather than applying universal rules.

Virtue ethics

Virtue ethics focus on the virtue or moral character of the researcher rather than principles, rules or consequences of an act or decision. Virtue ethics draw on the notion of researcher integrity and seek to identify the characteristics or virtues that a researcher needs in order to behave in morally (or ethically) 'good' ways.

Ethical regulation

Most research conducted by researchers in the UK and North America, and much research conducted in other European countries and indeed in the Western world, is subject to ethical regulation. The form this takes is review by a recognised ethics committee.

Ethical guidelines

Professional ethical guidelines and codes provide frameworks to enable researchers to think through the ethical dilemmas and challenges that they encounter in their research. In most cases, these guidelines are very general and with the exception of some specific issues such as confidentiality or matters that might result in accusations of research misconduct, they do not provide answers to how researchers should manage the specific situations that they might encounter in their research. Social researchers in many (but not all) disciplines can, and do, conduct research without being members of a professional organisation. It is also the case that guidelines are not legally enforceable. Nevertheless, a researcher may be excluded from membership of a professional organisation, damage their reputation and have difficulty getting their work published or gaining grants if they disregard these guidelines in ways that challenge disciplinary norms of ethical behaviour.

Informed consent

Informed consent involves providing participants with clear information about what participating in a research project will involve and giving them the opportunity to decide whether or not they want to participate.

Capacity

The term 'capacity' or 'competence' is used to refer to people's ability to give consent to participate in research. There are some groups for whom questions of capacity or 'competence' to provide consent are raised. These groups include children and young people, people with intellectual disability and people with some physical and/or mental illness and disability. People are assumed to lack capacity to consent if they are not able to understand what participating in research will involve, to weigh up the risks and benefits to them of participating or to reach their own decision about this and/or other matters that affect their life. Assessing capacity to consent is, in many cases, a judgement made by researchers but there are some legal issues that need consideration and specific issues are relevant for research with children and young people.

Duty of confidentiality

In the research context, the duty of confidentiality is taken to mean that identifiable information about individuals collected during the process of research will not be disclosed. Additionally, the duty of confidentiality may mean that specific information provided in the process of research will not be used at all if the participant requests this. Confidentiality is closely connected with anonymity. However, anonymisation of data does not cover all the issues raised by concerns about confidentiality.

Anonymity

The primary way that researchers seek to protect research participants from the accidental breaking of confidentiality is through the process of anonymisation, which occurs through the use of pseudonyms applied to research participants, organisations and locations or other ways of not revealing participants' real identities.

Risk

Ensuring the safety and well-being of research participants is an important element of ethical research practice. While much qualitative research may pose only minimal risks to participants, it is important not to disregard the risks that can occur, particularly in research on topics which are in some way 'sensitive' because they focus on personal issues, taboo issues or issues which pose a threat for those participating in it. Assessments of risk should also focus on risks for researchers which may arise from lone working or from the nature of the research.

2 Thinking ethically: approaches to research ethics

Introduction

Researchers inevitably experience ethical issues in the process of conducting research. Sometimes these issues are anticipated and planned for and may form part of decision making about a project before it commences. However, often ethical challenges and dilemmas are unexpected and emerge as research unfolds. While there are a number of 'common' ethical issues, and the following three chapters in this book explore these, research is always situated and contextual and the specific issues that arise are often unique to the context in which each individual research project is conducted. However, while ethical issues are often unique to a specific context, the management of such issues nevertheless needs to be informed by a range of ethical frameworks, approaches, regulation and guidelines. In this chapter the various guidelines, approaches and frameworks that inform, guide, and in some cases constrain, ethical decision-making, are outlined. An understanding of these provides an important basis from which researchers can think through, and argue, their ethical decisions.

The development of contemporary research ethics

Contemporary understanding of research ethics in social research has its roots in the history of medical research. The Nuremberg Code (1947) was developed as a result of the Nuremberg trials after the Second World War at which abuses to research subjects arising from experimentation by Nazi doctors were identified. The code set out ten key principles to underpin medical and experimental research, central to which were issues of consent and avoidance of risk to research participants. The World Health Organisation's Declaration of Helsinki (1964) developed this code and has been identified as central in subsequent legislation and ethical codes of conduct (Israel and Hay, 2006). However, despite the existence of these codes, further cases of abuse arising from medical and scientific research conducted during the 1960s and 1970s occurred. The most well known of these cases is the Tuskegee syphilis study which took place between 1932 and 1972, in which the effects of syphilis in 400 poor African-American men were studied over a prolonged period even though treatment for the disease had become available. This was not an isolated case and a number of other ethical scandals relating to biomedical studies were identified in which people were experimented on to examine disease progression and/ or to develop medical treatments (see Israel and Hay, 2006). It was the Tuskegee study in particular that has been identified as being instrumental in establishing the United States' National Commission for the Protection of Human Subjects in Biomedical and Behavioural Research in 1979 and the subsequent Belmont Report and the formation of Institutional Review Boards (IRBs) for reviewing research in the US. The Belmont Report (1979) has been highly influential and provides the underlying principles by which research ethics committees across the Western world evaluate research proposals. It identified three key principles, respect for persons, beneficence and justice, to which Beauchamp and Childress (1979), in a widely used book in the field of bioethics, added a fourth, that of non-maleficence (Macfarlane, 2009). These principles are discussed further here.

The ethical frameworks used in social research have emerged from the frameworks developed in relation to medical research. This is an issue that is a concern for many social scientists who view the risks of social research to be far less significant than for medical research. Nevertheless, it is important to recognise that the social sciences have not been immune from accusations of unethical behaviour. Stanley Milgram's (1963) obedience to authority experiment, Phillip Zimbardo's (see Haney, Banks and Zimbardo, 1973) Stanford prison experiment and Laud Humphreys' (1975) study on homosexual behaviour are commonly-cited ethical 'horror stories' in the social sciences.

The regulation of social research has increased significantly over the last decade, particularly in Europe and North America. In the USA, Institutional Review Boards (IRBs) have, since the 1970s, screened research on and with 'human subjects'. Their powers have been identified as considerable and wide ranging and their scope increasing (Haggerty, 2004). In the UK, funding bodies, such as the Economic and Social Research Council (ESRC), have established ethical frameworks (ESRC, 2005, 2010) resulting in the widespread formation of research ethics committees in universities and other research organisations (Tinker and Coomber, 2004). Research ethics committees had already been operating for some time for researchers conducting research in UK health care settings and, more recently, for research in social care. Similar developments have occurred in the European context, for example for research funded by the European Commission (Wiles, Clark and Prosser, 2011).

The result of these developments is that virtually all research conducted by researchers in the UK and North America, and much research conducted in other European countries and indeed in the Western world, is subject to some form of ethical review by a recognised ethics committee. This 'ethics creep' is viewed as moving UK, and other European, social research in the direction of the highly regulated system of review by IRBs in the US and is a development that has been widely criticised by UK social scientists (Dingwall, 2008; Hammersley, 2009) as well as social scientists in other countries (Israel and Hay, 2006). Concerns have been raised by researchers that increasing levels of review will encourage uniform approaches to 'ethical' issues such as anonymity and consent that avoid any level of risk; this has been identified as threatening the future of good quality social research and posing particular difficulties for researchers using ethnographic approaches (Murphy and Dingwall, 2007), online (Orton-Johnson, 2010), visual and creative methods (Prosser and Loxley, 2008) and approaches that involve the use of covert methods (Spicker, 2011). However, despite widespread concerns, it is highly likely that the ethical regulation of social research through research ethics committees will continue. Alongside critics of the system, various other authors have identified the importance of researchers engaging with systems of review to ensure committees are informed methodologically and ethically (Iphofen, 2009; Israel and Hay, 2006: 141; Pauwels, 2008; Wiles, Clark and Prosser, 2011). This is a position with which this book aligns itself. Iphofen (2009), among others, has noted that ethical review has an important educative function and one which does not of itself limit social research.

Ethical decision-making

Consideration of the links, overlaps and differences between morals, ethics, ethical approaches, ethical frameworks, ethical regulation and legal regulation are an important starting point for thinking about ethics.

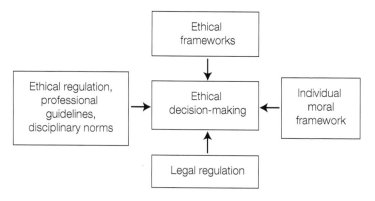

Figure 1 Factors shaping ethical decision-making in research

The decisions that researchers make about the ethical issues that they anticipate encountering in the research planning stage and those that emerge as research unfolds are influenced by several issues: professional guidelines; disciplinary norms; ethical and legal regulation and an individual's ethical and moral outlook. Figure 1 illustrates this diagrammatically. Each of these issues is explored in this chapter.

All individuals have a moral outlook about what is right and wrong that guides their behaviour. This moral outlook is shaped by individuals' experiences and interactions and the specific moral beliefs held are inevitably individual (see Gregory, 2003). Nevertheless, society has a large amount of agreement on specific moral *principles* about right and wrong (such as justice and fairness), even though there is considerable disagreement about the application of these principles to particular circumstances and contexts. Ethical approaches are the application of key moral norms (or principles). Ethical behaviour in research demands that researchers engage with moral issues of right and wrong. To do this they draw on ethical principles identified by the research community to which they belong. The specific ethical issues that researchers identify in their research are informed by their own moral outlook and their understanding of ethics in research. The frameworks for thinking about and managing them are informed largely by the ethical principles derived from the various approaches to ethics which are set out in professional ethical guidelines as well as various textbooks on the topic. Some of these ethical issues can be considered prior to the research commencing but many are emergent and become apparent only as the research proceeds. Researchers can draw on a range of resources from the literature and the research community to assist their thinking in how to manage such issues. It is crucial that they resolve the issues in ways that accord with their moral beliefs but also in ways that do not contravene the established ethical standards of their profession. Researchers' ethical decision-making is also strongly influenced by ethical and legal regulation. Researchers are legally obliged to conform with legal regulation relating to their research. Ethical regulation does not carry such weight but nevertheless researchers are generally obliged to comply with ethical regulation by their institution or by the organisations they are conducting research with or for. It should be noted that conforming with ethical or legal regulation does not necessarily equate with ethical (or moral) behaviour; compliance with regulation in many contexts is often the minimum requirement and ethical behaviour demands more careful consideration of the issues involved. These frameworks, guidelines and regulation that impact on ethical decision-making are explored here.

Ethical frameworks

A range of approaches to research ethics can be identified (see Israel and Hay, 2006; Macfarlane, 2009; Merten and Ginsberg, 2009). These approaches or frameworks provide a means of thinking about moral behaviour. They provide some criteria against which researchers can consider what it is right or wrong to do when presented with an ethical dilemma. These frameworks do not provide clear answers to such dilemmas but rather a means of thinking about them and assessing what an appropriate and defensible course of action might be. Consideration of these frameworks is therefore important in helping to guide researchers in thinking through the ethical challenges with which they are confronted. One of the challenges of engaging with these frameworks is that the criteria that each uses to inform moral decisions vary and thus the decisions that researchers may make will differ according to which framework is used. It is also the case that some of the criteria (or principles) *within* certain frameworks may lead people to reach different decisions about the ethical challenges they encounter according to which principle within a framework they give primacy to. The most common approaches are consequentialist, principlist, non-consequentialist, ethics of care and virtue ethics.

Consequentialist approaches argue that ethical decisions should be based on the consequences of specific actions so that an action is morally right if it will produce a good outcome for an individual or for wider society. In consequentialism, the more 'good' consequences that result from an act, the better or more right is the act; no act is seen as inherently *wrong* as judgements are based on the outcome of the act. Using a consequentialist approach, a researcher would assess what the outcome of a specific decision might be and decide on an action that they believe would result in the most beneficial outcome. For example, a researcher might argue that it would be acceptable to undertake covert visual research, for example on youth crime, if the findings of the research could be seen as benefiting society as a whole. Similarly, a researcher might argue that it is morally right to disclose confidential data from one participant if that might lead to a better outcome for a larger group of people. An example of consequentialist arguments is provided by Laud Humphreys' (1975) study of homosexual behaviour. This research has been widely criticised for being unethical but was defended by Humphreys on consequentialist grounds. Humphreys argued that increasing knowledge about homosexual behaviour was essential to bringing about a change in repressive laws and attitudes and that 'his ends justify the means' (Warwick 1982: 56). Further detail about Laud Humphreys' study is provided in chapter 6.

People using non-consequentialist approaches argue that consideration of matters other than the ends produced by actions need to be considered and that ethical decisions should be based on notions of what it is morally right to do regardless of the consequences. A researcher adopting a non-consequentialist approach might, for example, argue that it is morally right to maintain a confidence even if the consequences of that might not be beneficial or in the interests of the wider society. Principlist approaches are a form of non-consequentialist approach (see Beauchamp and Childress, 2001). This approach draws on the principles of respect for people's autonomy, beneficence, non-maleficence and justice in making and guiding ethical decisions in research. Respect for autonomy relates to issues of voluntariness, informed consent, confidentiality and anonymity. Beneficence concerns the responsibility to do good, non-maleficence concerns the responsibility to avoid harm and justice concerns the importance of the benefits and burdens of research being distributed equally. People using principlist approaches make ethical decisions on the basis of these specific principles. Central to a principlist approach is that consent must be freely given and that potential participants should not be subject to any encouragement (or coercion) to take part such as that arising from payment for participation or power relations between researcher and participant. Each of the principles is viewed as important but it is recognised that they may conflict with each other and in such cases it is necessary to make a case for why one might need to be chosen over another. Principlist approaches are widely used and commonly form the basis of evaluation of applications for ethical approval by research ethics committees (Israel and Hay, 2006: 37).

An ethics of care approach was originally identified by Carol Gilligan (1982) and has been developed by other feminist theorists (Mauthner *et al*, 2002; Held, 2006). In this approach, ethical decisions are made on the basis of care, compassion and a desire to act in ways that benefit the individual or group who are the focus of research, recognising the relationality and interdependency of researchers and research participants. This contrasts with the approaches outlined above which involve using rules or principles to address ethical dilemmas. An ethics of care approach means that researchers make decisions about ethical issues in relation to a particular case and by drawing on the notion of 'care' in relation to research participants, rather than applying universal rules. Held (2006) has identified some key features of the approach and argues that it involves: meeting the needs of others; recognising emotions; recognising people's relationality and interdependence; and respecting and seeking the views of others and their moral claims. This is an approach used in much feminist and participatory research where researchers develop close relationships with their participants (see Edwards and Mauthner, 2002). It has been viewed by some as a form of virtue ethics (see below) in that researchers need to develop particular characteristics or virtues in relation to the research they conduct. Mauthner *et al* (2002) have developed some guidelines for a feminist ethics of care which draws on the key features identified above. These comprise questions for researchers to consider in deliberating on ethical dilemmas (Mauthner *et al*, 2002: 28).

Virtue ethics is person-based; it focuses on the virtue or moral character of the researcher rather than principles, rules or consequences of an act or decision. Virtue ethics draws on the notion of researcher integrity and seeks to identify the characteristics or virtues that a researcher needs in order to behave in morally (or ethically) 'good' ways. Macfarlane (2009: 42) has identified the demands that different phases of the research process places on researchers and the moral virtues that researchers need to manage these challenges at each stage. He also identifies the corresponding 'vices' that characterise a deficit or excess of each virtue that researchers may exhibit when they fall short of a desired virtue. The virtues identified are courage, respectfulness, resoluteness, sincerity, humility and reflexivity. It is recognised that these virtues are ideals which researchers strive for and that the vices are what can occur when these ideals cannot be met. As Macfarlane notes (2009: 42), 'This set of virtues and vices represent the ideal character of the researcher and the temptations they face during what is a demanding social and intellectual process'. In relation to ethical dilemmas, a virtue ethics approach would expect a researcher to ask what a virtuous researcher would do in the given situation.

An ethical dilemma, based on one from my own experience, may help to clarify the actions that might be taken on the basis of these different frameworks. An ethical dilemma commonly experienced by researchers relates to the issue of confidentiality. For example, a case study I was involved in focusing on a new model of in-patient care in one hospital ward involved interviews with all staff and some patients to find out their views about the benefits and challenges of the new way of working. Interviews revealed that some staff lacked commitment to the new model of care and that this risked the success of the scheme. Should other people in the 'case' be informed that there were problems with staff commitment to the scheme so that these issues could be addressed or should I not intervene, given that to do so would involve breaches of confidentiality? A consequentialist would look to the possible outcomes of acting and perhaps would argue that the greatest good would come from disclosing this information in order to improve the efficacy of the scheme. A principlist would be likely to argue that upholding the principle of confidentiality should be paramount and that information should not be disclosed. An ethics of care approach would look to the impact of disclosing information on the participants who had provided it and would explore what the most beneficial outcome would be for them. A virtue ethics approach would explore what a 'virtuous' researcher would do in this context which would ensure *all* participants were treated with respect. In this case this would be likely to mean maintaining confidentiality.

These ethical frameworks provide researchers with the tools to guide decision-making in research. However, there are a range of other factors which shape, influence or constrain ethical decision-making. These are discussed here.

Legal, regulatory and professional frameworks

Professional ethical guidelines

There are many professional guidelines and codes aimed at providing frameworks to enable researchers to think through the ethical challenges that they encounter in their research (see for example, American Sociological Association, 1999; Association of Social Anthropologists, 2011; British Psychological Society, 2009; British Sociological Association, 2002; European Science Foundation, 2011; RESPECT guidelines, 2004; Social Research Association, 2003). There are also specific guidelines and codes on particular methods or approaches which raise ethical challenges, such as online research (Ess *et al*, 2002; British Psychological Society, 2007) and visual methods (British Sociological Association Visual Sociology Group's statement of ethical practice, 2006). These guidelines shape the decisions that researchers make about procedural and emergent ethical issues. They are drawn, to varying degrees, from the ethical approaches outlined above, particularly principlist approaches. Such guidelines are necessarily very general. Except in relation to some very specific issues, such as confidentiality or matters that might result in accusations of research misconduct, they do not provide answers to how researchers should manage the specific situations that they might encounter in their research. Rather, they outline principles to enable researchers to think through the specific situations that occur (Wiles *et al*, 2006). These guidelines recognise the situated and contextual nature of the ethical challenges that arise when conducting research. The principles addressed in these codes generally relate to issues of the well-being and rights of research participants, informed consent, privacy, confidentiality and anonymity. Social researchers in many disciplines can, and do, conduct research without being members of a professional organisation; as such not all researchers are subject to the guidelines and even if they are, these are not legally enforceable. Nevertheless, a researcher may be excluded from membership of a professional organisation, damage their reputation and have difficulty getting their work published or gaining grants if they disregard these guidelines in ways that challenge disciplinary norms of ethical behaviour. They might also be subject to disciplinary sanctions if they do not comply with institutional requirements of ethical research behaviour.

Ethical regulation

Most researchers are subject to ethical review procedures through a research ethics committee (REC). Committees vary widely in the ways in which they assess applications for review and the conclusions they come to, even in highly regulated and established systems such as that for the review of research in the UK National Research Ethics Service (Edwards *et al*, 2004; Israel, 2004). However, the general principles they assess are fairly uniform and are likely to comprise voluntary informed consent, the confidentiality of information provided by participants, the anonymity of study participants, the avoidance of harm and researcher integrity. These are issues that researchers are advised to consider carefully in preparing applications to RECs. RECs have the power to determine the way that various ethical issues will be managed within a research project. RECs generally focus on procedural or anticipated ethical issues; it appears that social researchers, in the UK at least, tend not to seek advice from RECs on ethical issues that emerge once research has commenced unless they are obliged to do so (Wiles *et al*, 2012). As noted above, some concerns have been raised that ethical regulation places limitations on research, particularly certain types of research such as ethnography, online research and visual methods.

Many resources exist to assist researchers through the ethical review process (see for example http://www.ethicsguidebook.ac.uk/). As well as the importance of preparing a good application that addresses the central ethical issues, researchers can adopt other strategies to maximise their chances of gaining approval. These include finding out how a local REC operates, opting for a committee that might be sympathetic, identifying a committee member to champion the application and being prepared to discuss the application with committee members (Wiles *et al*, 2012; Israel and Hay, 2006). While RECs have considerable power in determining how ethical issues will be managed in research, there is some evidence that researchers have developed ways to work with ethics committees to modify their impact (Wiles *et al*, 2012).

Legal regulation

Research is subject to a number of legal considerations with which researchers are obliged to comply. When considering legal issues it is important to bear in mind that these provide a framework of the minimum standards that need to be adhered to but that these, by themselves, do not necessarily equate with ethical or moral practice. Masson (2004: 43) notes:

> There is a close relationship between law and ethics but not everything that is legal is ethical. Frequently law … attempts only to set the minimum acceptable standard. The aspirations of ethical practice are higher … It can never be appropriate to defend proposed practice solely on the basis that it is legal.

Specific laws vary across countries but similar laws exist in most Western countries. The following refers primarily to the situation in the UK unless otherwise stated. There are a number of laws that have a bearing on research; these relate to consent, confidentiality, privacy, data protection and copyright. The information given here does not constitute legal advice and researchers with specific concerns should seek legal advice from their institution. More detailed information on the UK legal issues identified here can be found on the Ethics Guidebook website (http://www.ethics-guidebook.ac.uk).

In the UK, adults who lack the capacity to make the decision whether or not to participate in research are covered by the Mental Capacity Act or the Adults with Incapacity (Scotland) Act. The Act applies to all people who lack the capacity to make a decision at the time it is sought, whether or not the lack of capacity is permanent or temporary. Researchers undertaking research with adults who lack the capacity to consent must have their ethics application approved by a medical or social care research ethics committee who will assess the validity of the project and the necessity of people with limited capacity being involved in it.

The law around the process of consent for children under the age of sixteen to participate in research is complex. Children who are able to understand the implications of participation in a research study are viewed as having the 'capacity' to make a decision about whether or not to take part in research. Parental consent is needed if a child is not viewed as having the capacity to consent. However, in practice, researchers often seek parental consent (in addition to children's consent) regardless of a child's capacity to consent in order to safeguard them from any problems that might arise. These issues are explored in more detail in chapter 3. In line with UK legislation, Criminal Records Bureau (CRB) checks are also necessary for researchers working with children and with other groups deemed 'vulnerable'.

There is no specific legislation relating to confidentiality in the UK but there is a common law duty of confidentiality such that there is an expectation that information given in confidence to a researcher will not be disclosed without prior consent. There are, however, situations in which commitments to confidentiality can be overridden. Failure of a researcher to take appropriate action in cases where a child discloses that they are being seriously harmed or mistreated could result in legal liability. In the UK, people who suspect a child is being mistreated are not legally obliged to report this. However, a range of professionals (such as teachers and social workers) are obliged to do so under Local Authority child protection procedures. There is no law regarding actions in the case of data relating to less serious crime and researchers are left to make their own decisions on appropriate actions, if any. In the case of adults, there is no law that obliges researchers to pass data on adults engaged in criminal activity to the legal authorities. However, researchers should be aware that research data given in confidence do not enjoy legal privilege and they may be liable to subpoena by a court (Wiles, Crow *et al* 2008). There are no cases of this occurring in the UK but cases have been reported in other countries. These issues are discussed further in chapter 4.

There are no privacy laws in the UK but Article 8 of the European Convention of Human Rights protects the right to respect for private and family life, home and correspondence. Observing, photographing or filming someone in a place where they might have a reasonable expectation of privacy, or indeed using personal data, might be considered an invasion of privacy. Additionally, researchers are also subject to the Data Protection Act which demands that data are kept securely and do not lead to any breach of agreed confidentiality and anonymity.

Copyright law is of relevance to researchers using still or moving images. Copyright rests with the person taking the image, or their employing institution. A research participant who agrees to have their photograph taken or be subject to video recording has no legal rights over the subsequent use of their image. This also applies to the archiving and reuse of visual data. In the case of respondent-generated visual data (for example, photos a study participant has taken), copyright rests with the respondent and it is necessary for them to assign copyright to the researcher for their subsequent use in a research project (Wiles, Prosser *et al*, 2008). Issues of copyright are also relevant in relation to online research where clear citation of internet sources must be provided and permission given for the use of images.

Making ethical decisions

How can these ethical frameworks, guidance and regulation be used in practice in making decisions about ethical issues that are anticipated prior to a study commencing or that emerge throughout the process of research? There are various resources which provide researchers with advice about managing the 'standard' ethical issues that need to be addressed in the process of obtaining approval from a research ethics committee (see, for example, Iphofen, 2009). In preparing applications for committees, researchers obviously have to draw on the various frameworks, guidance and regulation outlined above. Committees also play a role in monitoring and advising on the management of ethical issues at the anticipatory stage of research. More challenging are the ethical issues that emerge during the process of conducting research. Such challenges are often unique to the context of a research project, are unexpected and unplanned for; researchers are often presented with an ethical issue for which they feel ill-prepared and unsure about how best to resolve.

Various strategies exist that researchers use to manage such ethical challenges. The strategies that researchers use to make decisions draw on various elements of the frameworks outlined above, although researchers' deliberations may not always involve a conscious engagement with these frameworks. Often researchers may resolve their ethical dilemmas by drawing on their moral judgement about the appropriate course of action but this is invariably one that is informed by ethical frameworks. While researchers may argue that research is situated and contextual and that ethical dilemmas cannot be resolved by appeal to higher principles and codes, the argument presented in this book is that an understanding of moral codes and principles does not force researchers into specific pre-determined decisions but rather assists them in making sound, justifiable ethical decisions.

Various models to guide decision-making in the face of ethical challenges have been identified. Israel and Hay (2006: 132), for example, outline a seven-step process involving: i) identifying the nature of the problem and the stakeholders involved; ii) identifying various options for resolving the dilemmas; iii) identifying the range of consequences of each option for different stakeholders; iv) considering the short and long-term implications of decisions; v) considering the options by reference to moral principles such as honesty, trust, autonomy, fairness and equality; vi) integrating consequences and principles to reach an independent and justifiable decision; vii) reflecting on the decision. Israel and Hay (2006: 135) provide a number of questions that researchers can ask themselves as part of the process of reflecting on the morality of the proposed action to be taken to resolve the ethical dilemma:

> Several prompts can be used to reflect on the action that is about to be adopted. MacDonald (2002) urges us to consider the following: will I feel comfortable telling a close family member such as my mother or father what I have done; how would I feel if my actions were to attract media attention; how would I feel if my children followed my example; and is mine the behaviour of a wise and virtuous person?

A similar model is proposed by Kitchener and Kitchener (2009: 9) who identify the different levels of reasoning that underpin ethical decision-making. They note that researchers can move up through the levels according to the complexity of the decision. At level 1 is a researcher's moral sense which is informed by their beliefs and values. At level 2 are the various ethical codes and disciplinary frameworks which guide moral decision-making and which form the 'accumulated wisdom' of a profession or discipline. If ethical dilemmas cannot be resolved at these levels, they need to be critically evaluated in relation to ethical principles such as beneficence, non-maleficence, honesty and fairness to reach a sound and justifiable ethical decision.

Summary

This chapter has outlined the various guidelines, approaches and frameworks that inform, and in some cases constrain, ethical decision-making. These include ethical frameworks, professional guidelines and ethical and legal regulation. An understanding of these provides an important basis from which researchers can think through, and argue the case for, their ethical decisions.

3 Informed consent

Introduction

Informed consent is a central concept in ethical research practice and is one of the key principles underpinning professional guidelines for social scientists (see for example, British Psychological Society, 2009; British Sociological Association, 2002; Social Research Association, 2003). It involves providing participants with clear information about what participating in a research project will involve and giving them the opportunity to decide whether or not they want to participate. Specifically, research participants need to be made aware of: what the research is about; why it is being conducted; who is funding it; what will happen to the results and how they will be disseminated; what their participation in the project will involve; what the potential risks and benefits of their involvement might be; and, how issues of anonymity and confidentiality will be managed. Potential research participants should also be made aware that they are not obliged to take part and that they can withdraw from the study if they later change their mind about participating.

While at first glance informed consent may appear a relatively straightforward issue, a closer examination of the issues involved reveals that the process is far from straightforward. Social researchers have to balance a number of factors in managing issues of informed consent. Obviously they have to comply with any legal frameworks and regulation as discussed in chapter 2 but additionally they have to balance a range of sometimes competing interests, such as the aims of the research, what they consider to be the best interests of research participants as well as the interests of formal or informal gatekeepers. They also have to operationalise and be reflexive about issues of 'information', 'consent' and 'competence'. This chapter explores general issues of informed consent as they apply to qualitative research across methodological approaches.

Notions of informed consent imply that participants will always be fully informed about what participating in research will involve. While recognising that intentions to 'fully inform' participants may be problematic, which is discussed below, it is also important to note that there are some research projects in which participants cannot be fully informed about the research before it takes place; to do so would render the research impossible to undertake. Various research projects in psychology, for example, explore behaviour in specific contexts that would change if study participants were made aware of the aims of the study. In research projects such as these, participants are consented to the research on the basis of limited or false information about the study aims but they should always be fully debriefed after the data have been collected and at this point be given full information about the study and have the opportunity to give full consent for their data to be used; they would be expected to have the right to withdraw themselves, and their data, from the study if they wished to do so. In the light of concerns raised about unethical experiments conducted by social psychologists in the 1960s and 70s, such as the well-known Milgram experiment on obedience to authority and the Stanford Prison experiment (see http://www.experiment-resources.com/milgram-experiment-ethics.html), there are very strict ethical controls on how informed consent is managed in studies when some level of deception is necessary for the research to be conducted (see British Psychological Society, 2009).

Covert research is another type of research in which informed consent prior to the research commencing is not possible. There have been some important studies which have conducted research covertly, particularly in the area of criminology. Typical examples are studies of football hooligans, of neo-Nazi groups and of corporate activities (see Scratton, 2004). Some proponents of covert research have argued that it is in the interests of the general public to expose how some organisations or institutions operate and, in some cases, the only way this can occur is through covert means. However, various criticisms of covert research have been raised including that it violates the principle of informed consent, invades privacy, betrays trust and 'spoils the field' for other researchers (for a discussion of these issues see Herrera, 1999; Homan and Bulmer, 1982; Homan, 1991; Punch, 1986; Spicker, 2011). In the face of increasing ethical regulation of research, research conducted completely covertly has become relatively rare. Nevertheless, it is still the case that much research, while not expressly covert, may take place without participants being fully aware of to what they are consenting. The challenges to achieving informed consent in research that aims to do so are the focus of the rest of this chapter.

Providing information

The provision of information about a project is an important part of ensuring that potential participants understand what participating in a research project might entail. However, many issues need to be taken into consideration in making decisions about this; these include how much information to provide, when to provide it and how often to repeat it. In terms of the *amount* of information to provide, it is clearly important to provide comprehensive information about the project so that participants can understand what being a participant will involve for them. However, giving very comprehensive information that runs to several pages is likely to be very offputting; not only are people unlikely to read it or take it in, it also risks putting them off participating. Ethical regulation, particularly for research conducted in health care settings and subject to review by the National Research Ethics Service (NRES), may pose severe restrictions on researchers' ability to provide information in a non-standard way. The same applies to research reviewed by Institutional Review Boards (IRBs) in the US.

Consideration of *how* information is provided is also important. It is obviously crucial that information is presented in a user-friendly way. This involves giving consideration to the layout, colour, size of text, type of language and the inclusion of graphics in the provision of information. For researchers working with children, young people or groups with limited comprehension, innovative ways often need to be identified to engage with participants to enable them to understand what participating in a study might involve. This is likely to involve keeping written information to a minimum and incorporating pictures and other graphics into the information provided. Researchers have experimented with a range of ways of providing information to meet these needs including the use of photos, comic strips and video (Clarke *et al*, 2011).

A further practical issue involves consideration of *when* to provide information. In some research contexts, particularly if the research is complex, it may be appropriate to provide some introductory information to potential participants about the research and to provide full information only if they express an interest in participating. This is one way of dealing with potential information overload for participants. In longitudinal studies or research with repeated stages of data collection it may be appropriate to provide information, and gain consent, for each stage of data collection to ensure that participants give their continuing consent to participate in the study. This approach highlights the importance of viewing consent as a process that is ongoing throughout a project rather than as a one-off event that occurs when recruiting people to a study. Some researchers, regardless of the type of study or its methodology, view adopting a model of 'process consent' as appropriate, in which consent is discussed and negotiated throughout the whole period of a study, because it ensures that participants are truly giving informed consent (Goodenough *et al*, 2004; Cameron *et al*, 2004; Cutliffe and Ramcharan, 2002). This is an approach adopted particularly by researchers working in participatory research paradigms. Renold *et al* (2008) provide a good example of this approach in their study of the everyday lives and identities of children in care in which consent was negotiated at all stages of the project:

> Children's 'consent' forms (requested by the university ethics committee) were purposively constructed as open-ended, partial and provisional, ensuring that children and young people could choose how to engage in a research project. Our overall aim was to use a language that framed their participation as always negotiable. For example, they could choose whether or not they wished to sign the consent form and a designated part of the leaflet was formed in which they could outline their own expectations or desires about the project and our own role as researchers ... our approach [was] to engage in an ongoing dialogue from the outset, which involved developing personalized ethical protocols 'in the moment' with children and young people. (Renold *et al*, 2008: 443)

Underlying these practical issues of how much information to give, how to present it and when and how often to give it, are a number of challenges inherent in the research process which give rise to ethical dilemmas that impact on the decisions that researchers make about these issues. The first is the difficulty in providing comprehensive information to research participants about a study. In qualitative research the specific focus and outcomes of a research study, and perhaps even the phases of data collection, are often not known at the start of a study as study design is generally emergent. So, for example, at the outset of a study, a general research focus or set of questions may have been designed but the number of study participants, the number of interviews to be carried out with each individual and the specific direction of the research is often dependent on the data collected and the emerging analysis. This is particularly the case for ethnographic research.

A related issue concerns the ways in which the data collected will be written up and disseminated in public arenas which is unlikely to be known at the start of a research project; indeed, the dissemination of research findings may continue for many years after the completion of a project. While researchers have varying views about whether or not consent should refer only to participation in a study rather than the way data are used in publications it is, nevertheless, an important issue for consideration in relation to consent and one which links closely to issues of anonymity and confidentiality and ownership of data. Clearly if data are in any sense 'owned' by participants (such as photographs they have taken) or if participants are potentially identifiable, then consent needs to be extended to the ways in which data are used. The point here is that the ability to give comprehensive information at the beginning of a study about what participating will involve for an individual and what will happen to the data produced is often impossible. It is also the case of course that it is impossible to know what participating in a research project will be like for specific individuals. Researchers cannot know what particular issues an individual might feel sensitive about or find distressing or what the experience of participating will be like for them. Various authors have noted that it is unlikely that participants can ever fully understand to what they are consenting and what researchers' intentions are (Miller and Bell, 2002; Prosser, 2000; Wiles *et al*, 2007). The best a researcher can do is to aim to give optimal information, to anticipate what risks could arise from the project and to inform participants of them, to consider the stages at which consent is necessary and to make plans for achieving such consent.

A second challenge inherent in the research process is that it is often difficult to provide information (and gain consent) from everyone involved in a research project. This is particularly the case when conducting research in public settings, such as at public events, in shopping malls, libraries, art galleries, schools or hospital waiting rooms. In such cases it might be possible to inform key individuals but providing detailed information to everyone who might be observed or in some way 'participate' in a study in a public setting is likely to be impractical if not impossible. It is generally the case that researchers attempt to inform people in public arenas that research is being undertaken by, for example, putting up posters informing people about a project and when data collection is taking place. This provides the possibility for individuals to remove themselves if they do not wish to 'participate', or, if practical, request that they are excluded from data collection. Even in research in less public settings, such as in people's homes, it can be the case that others contribute, such as in cases when a spouse or friends of a research participant are present during an interview and contribute to it. It is a moot point whether or not people who have contributed in a minor, and unexpected, way to a research project should be considered as participants for whom consent is needed. In general, this is likely to depend on the level of their involvement.

A third challenge involves the role of gatekeepers to research participants. Some research projects necessitate researchers gaining consent from various gatekeepers, such as managers, head-teachers or hospital consultants, before it is possible to approach the individuals who are to be invited to be research participants. While gatekeepers may need to give permission for individuals in their employ or care to be approached, this does not negate the need to seek consent from the specific individuals being invited to participate in a study. It may be that gatekeepers view themselves as able to consent for others they are responsible for, but researchers should ensure that in addition to gatekeeper approval, approval from individual participants is also sought. This can be difficult to do in some institutions where gatekeepers view themselves as in a position to give consent on behalf of those for whom they are responsible or who are in their care as may be the case in prisons or schools. Even if approached to give consent, the extent to which consent is freely and voluntarily given in contexts in which power dynamics form part of the relationship with the gatekeeper can be difficult; schools, prisons and residential institutions are clear examples where gaining consent from participants may be difficult because of a culture of compliance. In cases where someone in a powerful position in an organisation who has sanctioned a research project will know that an individual has refused to participate, it may feel that, in effect, an individual's choice whether or not to consent is limited. The onus is on researchers to identify ways in which research participants are enabled to make decisions whether or not to participate in research, free from any influence from gatekeepers.

This will involve researchers spending time with participants to explore their wishes. It may also involve identifying ways to keep their decisions confidential from gatekeepers. Heath *et al* (2009: 33) identify a range of strategies that researchers working in educational contexts have used to enable children and young people to decline to participate in research without their teacher's knowledge. These include providing alternative activities for participants to do when ostensibly participating in research. Research with children and other (so called) 'vulnerable groups' who are viewed as lacking the 'capacity' (or 'competence') to give consent raises related but specific issues, and these will be explored in a separate section in this chapter.

A fourth challenge concerns operationalising participants' right to withdraw from research. Part of informed consent concerns giving people the right to withdraw from their participation in a study at any point. This implies the need for researchers to ensure that they have people's ongoing consent to participate in a study (as discussed above) and that they are sensitive to recognising participants' expressions of desire to opt out of a study. It is generally expected that information sheets and consent forms would state that participants have the right to withdraw from a study at any stage. However, researchers have noted that it is common, particularly for some groups, to be reluctant to state they do not want to continue being involved with a project (Alderson, 2004). So, for example, children might find it difficult to tell an adult that they no longer want to participate in a study or that they do not want to answer a particular question. The same issue can apply to people in a range of contexts because of the power relations that can exist between the researcher and the researched or simply a lack of awareness that they can say no to something to which they have previously agreed. Researchers need to be vigilant to participants' unspoken expressions of reluctance to continue to participate during data collection, such as an apparent lack of interest or irritation with the data collection (see Langston *et al*, 2004; Rodgers, 1999). In research with children and people with limited communication, some researchers have used 'stop' cards that participants can hold up if they do not want to answer a particular question or no longer want to participate (Wiles *et al*, 2005). If this type of method is to be used it is important that participants practise using it before the data collection proper commences.

In reality, wholesale promises that participants can withdraw from a study at any time may be difficult to uphold and researchers need to think through the process whereby they can manage individual requests to withdraw from a study. It may be that enabling participants to withdraw is actually time-limited. While it may be straightforward for individuals to decline to participate in a specific phase of data collection, the withdrawal of data from an individual once analysis has taken place can be difficult, if not impossible. The limits to withdrawal from a study need to be made clear to research participants.

A final challenge is that, in some areas of research, people are often keen to take part because of an interest in the topic, because they do not want to appear unco-operative by saying 'no', because they are unaware of any risks that participation might involve or because they trust the researcher. In these cases, study participants often disregard researchers' explanations of what the research will involve or are reluctant to take the time needed to read information sheets properly. It can be very difficult to be sure that participants understand what they are consenting to in such contexts. One interviewee in a study on informed consent for example noted (Wiles *et al*, 2007: 6):

> We do what we can just to hold back young people's enthusiasm for taking part because on the whole most young people are very keen to take part and to be listened to... we as researchers can be sort of overwhelmed by young people's enthusiasm and just think "yeah they understand, fine let's get on"... "that's informed consent" and I, you know, I don't think it is... they just think "oh great, this sounds fun".

Encouraging participation: incentives, encouragement and acknowledgement

The issue of whether or not some form of recompense, either financial or material, should be given to research participants as part of the process of consent is a subject of some debate. Recompense can be viewed as an incentive or inducement that may offer considerable encouragement for some groups to participate in research, who might without the 'reward' offered decline to participate. On the other hand, some researchers view such 'rewards' to be a just recompense for the time and effort of being involved in a research study. Nevertheless, the issue of payments raises questions about the role of 'rewards' when these are offered as part of the information given to participants about a study and whether this impacts negatively on the extent to which informed consent can be freely given.

It is clearly important that study participants are not out of pocket as a result of participating in research; travel expenses and any expenses relating to loss of income as a result of participating in research cannot be seen as an undue inducement. Payments, or other rewards such as gift vouchers, might arguably be viewed in a different light. Decisions about offering 'rewards' of some type are hampered by the fact that some groups, particularly various professional groups, are unlikely to agree to participate in research unless they are paid for their time. This has led some researchers to the view that, in the interests of fairness, all research participants should be paid a fee, not just those who demand it. In relation to 'hard to reach' groups, who have been traditionally excluded from research, ways need to be identified to encourage participation and these might include some form of 'appropriate reward'. Whether or not the importance of gaining insight into these previously excluded groups should over-ride concerns about incentives would need consideration and justification. There is also the issue that some researchers, particularly those working in areas of deprivation and need, may view it as important to be able to 'give something back' to participants by way of acknowledging them for their time and effort. Such 'rewards' might be personal to an individual participant or to an organisation or community. In Smyth's (2004: 53) study on segregation in South Africa, for example, food was given to interview participants and a donation made to a local organisation that worked in the community. The challenges that 'rewards' for participation pose for informed consent can be offset by not informing participants that they will be paid until after they have agreed to participate. In this way, any payment or benefit becomes a 'thank you' for participating rather than an incentive. The difficulty with this is that it is not always possible to keep this a surprise when research takes place among a bounded group of participants, as word of mouth is likely to circulate quickly so a 'thank you' can soon become an incentive.

Recording consent

The process of gaining consent involves researchers obtaining evidence that participants have consented to take part in a research project and have an understanding of the key issues involved. Consent should cover a general agreement to participate as well as confirmation that participants understand how data will be recorded, how anonymity and confidentiality will be managed and how the study will be disseminated. If specific consent is needed for the use of material owned by participants and/or it is intended that data will be archived for secondary analysis, there should be a space for participants to indicate whether or not they consent to this. Where the research design is complex or where consent is sought for a range of different activities, a consent form should include options so that participants can give or withhold their consent for each of them.

Iphofen (2009: 74) notes that consent 'should be gained in the most convenient, least disturbing manner for both researcher and researched'. In practice it is common that researchers use signed consent forms; indeed, with the rise of ethical regulation signed consent forms have become the norm in social research. The perceived advantages of using signed consent forms are that they increase the likelihood that participants understand what participation involves and that they protect the researcher from any subsequent complaints from study participants (Coomber 2002). However, asking an individual for a signature can be problematic in some research contexts, particularly in research that relates to socially unacceptable behaviour or where participants need protection. Researchers such as Coomber (2002) and the Domestic Violence Research Group (2004) have noted that the use of signed consent forms may compromise issues of confidentiality and anonymity which are important issues where participants are in need of protection. Participants may fear that signed consent forms may make the information they provide traceable to them which may put them at risk of physical harm (in the context of research topics such as domestic violence) or vulnerable to potential investigation and prosecution by the criminal justice system (in the case of illegal activities). Coomber (2002) has noted that individuals may want to protect their identities from the researcher and expecting them to divulge it runs counter to other ethical principles. He notes that individuals involved in illegal activities who are asked to sign consent forms are unlikely to want to participate in research and, if they do so, they are likely to give a false name, thereby making the process meaningless. Furthermore, Coomber notes that signed consent forms are not in the interests of researchers as they may force them to be complicit in the prosecution of research participants which would contravene researchers' responsibilities to participants.

Additionally, signed consent is problematic when working with people who are illiterate or have language or communication problems or indeed when working with people who do not have good command of the language in which the research is taking place. It is also the case that the need to obtain a signature in other contexts might be problematic in that it makes the process a formal one and this might be seen as off-putting for some people. Researchers have developed a range of ways of obtaining consent without the use of signatures which may be appropriate in some circumstances, such as the use of tape-recorded consent, providing marks on a consent form or, in the case of people with limited verbal communication skills, holding up red or green cards to indicate yes or no. While the opportunities to use alternatives to signed consent forms may be limited by ethical regulation, nevertheless a case can be made, in certain circumstances, for different approaches to recording consent. The challenge for researchers is to find a way to record that study participants give their informed consent to participate in a project. Signed consent does not necessarily achieve this any better than other methods.

Consent in online research

Online research raises particular challenges for consent which differ according to the specific online research method being used. More detailed information on these issues can be found in Hooley *et al* (2012), Ess (2002) and on the Exploring Online Research Methods website, http://www.restore.ac.uk/orm/ethics/ethcontents.htm.

In relation to online interviews with people identified through personal contacts, online forums or discussion groups, consent can be gained through the use of a consent form, either in hard copy or electronic. One difficulty raised is that in the virtual world it is impossible to know if a study participant is who they say they are. Assessing their capacity to give informed consent may be difficult and it may not be possible to ascertain their age, status or vulnerability. More significant challenges in relation to informed consent are raised by online ethnography. There are often difficulties in identifying and providing information about research, and gaining consent, from all members of an online community who may be observed. As Hooley *et al* (2012) note, in online communities there are a small number of participants who are very active and a larger group who may interact with the community only sporadically but who remain part of the community. Maintaining on-going consent with what may be a changing group of participants is also problematic. Some researchers may view it as appropriate to observe behaviour in an online group without the consent of the participants. This might sometimes be done in the early stages of a research project when a researcher is seeking to understand how a community operates and how they might best introduce their research project to the group. This 'lurking' in online communities has been identified as unethical and potentially damaging to the group observed. While it may not be necessary to gain consent from all participants prior to observing an online group it is nevertheless essential that participants are aware of a researcher's identity and their interest in the group. Kozinets (2010: 148) has identified the central tenets of ethical research practice in online ethnography which include the need for researchers to openly identify themselves as researchers, to describe their research focus and how they will conduct their research with the group.

There are some types of information provided in online environments which are viewed as 'public' and for which consent for their use is perceived as unnecessary. This refers largely to postings for mass and public communications. There has been much debate about what is public and what is private on the internet and it is recognised that users may have varying views about the public or private nature of their contributions. It has been suggested that informed consent should always be sought for research focusing on communications which people view as private and which take place in private or semi-private forums but that this may not be essential in open access forums which are acknowledged and understood as public. The Association of Internet Researchers (Ess *et al*, 2002: 5) notes 'the greater the acknowledged publicity of the venue, the less obligation there may be to protect individual privacy, confidentiality and the right to informed consent'. See also chapter 7 for a discussion of these issues in relation to digital and e-research.

Capacity to consent

There are some groups for whom questions of capacity or 'competence' to provide consent are raised. These groups include children and young people, people with intellectual disability and people with some physical and/or mental illness and disability. These groups of people are sometimes referred to as 'vulnerable' in relation to research; however, different issues are raised in relation to consent according to the specific capacity issue that is raised. If people are not able to understand what participating in research will involve, to weigh up the risks and benefits to them of participating or to reach their own decision about this and/or other matters that affect their lives then they would be assumed to lack capacity. Specific issues are relevant for research with children and young people and these will be addressed below.

If research is being conducted in England and Wales with adults who lack the capacity to consent then the 2005 Mental Capacity Act applies. In accordance with the Act, researchers must consult with someone close to the individual to advise whether s/he would want to be involved with the study. In all cases proposals for the research need to be assessed by an approved NHS or social care Research Ethics Committee (see http://www.ethicsguidebook.ac.uk/Mental-Capacity-Act-118).

Assessing capacity to consent is, in many cases, a judgement made by researchers. Many researchers believe it is possible to explain research in ways that the great majority of participants, even young children and people with disabilities, can understand. This involves being sensitive to the needs of particular individuals, providing appropriate materials to help to explain the research and engaging with them in ways that suit their styles of communicating. Rodgers (1999: 428), for example, notes in her research with people with learning difficulties that 'given careful explanations, many people with learning disability can understand and make decisions'. Identifying ways in which individuals can indicate their wish to discontinue participating has also been identified as important and part of the issue of ongoing consent. This is likely to involve becoming familiar with the ways in which individuals convey assent and dissent. In relation to both of these points the ways in which this can be achieved is likely to be different for different groups and individuals.

Proxy consent, that is consent given by someone, usually a relative or carer, on behalf of someone else, is rarely used in social research. While a proxy may be approached to assist in understanding whether an individual would be willing to participate in research, it is generally viewed as important that the assent of the individual concerned is also attained, and that this is monitored over the timeframe of the research. Certainly, ethical review committees would want a strong justification for the use of proxy consent. As noted above, many researchers hold the view that it is generally possible to explain a study in ways that someone can understand whatever (within reason) their level of 'competence'. If this is not possible, including an individual in a study raises significant ethical concerns and needs a strong justification in accordance with the Mental Capacity Act.

Research with children and young people raises a different set of issues and there is considerable debate, and some uncertainty among researchers, about researchers' legal obligations. In practice, unless there is clear guidance, interpretations of the age of competence to consent are varied. In law, children are generally seen as not competent to make decisions (in various areas of life) until the age of sixteen, although this has been challenged through the legal distinction of Gillick-competent children (see http://www.nspcc.org.uk/inform/research/questions/gillick_wda61289. html).

Gillick-competency is based on the assumption that a young person under sixteen years of age with 'sufficient understanding' can provide consent in their own right and that their parent has no right to override their wishes. The Fraser Guidelines set out by Lord Fraser in his judgement of the Gillick case in the House of Lords relate specifically to contraceptive advice but are regarded as applicable to social research. They imply that children under the age of sixteen, providing they can demonstrate an understanding of research, are able to participate in a project without their parents' permission. Masson (2004) notes that if a researcher has not sought parental permission (or consent), they are not at risk of legal proceedings brought by parents unless a claim of harm was made by the child. It is important to note that only the prospective research participant can consent to take part in research. Parental 'consent' relates only to consent to approach the child. Obtaining parental permission for the child to be approached is therefore distinct from the ethical principle of consent. Nevertheless, it may be good practice to seek permission from parents if not to do so might lead to upset on the part of parents given researchers' responsibility not to cause distress in the process of conducting research (particularly from an ethics of care or virtue ethics perspective).

There are some areas of research in which researchers might view it as problematic for parental permission to be sought. Examples are sexual behaviour, personal relationships and drug use where young people might not want their parents to know about their involvement in specific behaviours or they might be concerned about the interest from their parents that involvement in the research might generate. Heath *et al* (2009: 27-28) provide some examples, both positive and negative, of the ways that research ethics committees have responded to researchers' proposals not to obtain permission from parents in research with young people on sensitive topics.

However, despite the Gillick ruling, many researchers do seek parental permission, as well as consent from children, for participation in research. Partly this is because establishing whether a young person has 'sufficient understanding' to give informed consent is problematic. An additional factor driving this is that institutional gatekeepers to children and young people tend to request parental permission (or consent) for children or young people to participate in research as a condition of gaining access. The advice from various guidelines in relation to research with children is that parental permission should generally be sought in order to protect children as well as researchers. However, this should always be in conjunction with consent from the children and young people themselves and parental wishes should not override those of the child; that is, if the parent gives permission but the child does not want to participate then they should be excluded from the research. A more problematic situation occurs if the parent refuses permission but the child wishes to participate.

Summary

Informed consent is not a straightforward concept. Obviously researchers must comply with any legal frameworks and regulation but additionally they have to balance a range of sometimes competing interests, such as the aims of the research, what they consider to be the best interests of research participants as well as the interests of formal or informal gatekeepers. They also have to operationalise and be reflexive about issues of 'information', 'consent' and 'competence'.

4 Anonymity and confidentiality

Introduction

Issues of anonymity and confidentiality are key considerations in ethical research practice and, in common with informed consent, are concepts that underpin professional research guidelines for social scientists. The management of confidentiality and anonymity is closely linked with the management of consent in that participants need to be informed about how confidentiality and anonymity will be managed and what the implications of taking part will be in relation to these issues before consenting to participate. In other words, they need to be made aware what will happen to the data, how they will be reported, whether it will be possible for them to be identified from these data and what the implications of that might be for them. Consideration of the implications of participating in relation to confidentiality and anonymity is something that the individual participant needs to assess in the light of their views about what is public and what is private and the risks involved. However, they need to be guided in this by the researcher who will know how the research will be disseminated and who the likely audiences will be.

The terms confidentiality and anonymity tend to be conflated in research but are in fact distinct but related concepts. Iphofen (2009: 91) usefully notes that confidentiality is a continuous variable in that some information is 'mundane' and does not need to be kept private while other information may be viewed as highly confidential by research participants and not for sharing with others. Anonymity, on the other hand, is a dichotomous variable – a person's identity is either anonymised or kept secret. Nevertheless, in most qualitative research, confidentiality (through the process of anonymity) cannot be assured; researchers can tell participants that they will endeavour to ensure that they are not able to be identified but they cannot guarantee this will be the case. While anonymisation of research participants has traditionally been the norm in

41

social research, there is an increasing awareness that research participants may want to be identified in research outputs. Indeed, in some types of research identification of research participants is accepted practice.

This chapter will discuss the concept of confidentiality in relation to social research and the situations in which deliberate and accidental breaches of confidentiality can occur. It will also explore processes of anonymisation and debates around the identification of research participants.

Confidentiality

Confidentiality is commonly understood as akin to the principles of privacy and respect for autonomy (Oliver, 2003; Gregory, 2003) and is taken to mean that information given to another person will not be repeated without their permission. In the research context, confidentiality is taken to mean that identifiable information about individuals collected during the process of research will not be disclosed and that the identity of research participants will be protected through various processes designed to anonymise them, unless they specifically choose to be identified. Additionally, confidentiality may mean that specific information provided in the process of research will not be used at all if the participant requests this (sometimes referred to as 'off the record' comments). The concept of confidentiality is closely connected with anonymity; in social research anonymity is the vehicle by which confidentiality is operationalised. However, anonymisation of data does not cover all the issues raised by concerns about confidentiality. Confidentiality of data also includes not deliberately or accidentally disclosing what has been said in the process of data collection with others in ways that might identify an individual. A deliberate breach of confidentiality would involve, for example, telling a parent what a child had said in an interview or telling a health professional what a patient participant had said without the study participant's consent. An accidental breach of confidentiality would involve, for example, someone being identified through information that a researcher provided about an individual even though they had not named them.

Breaking confidentiality

The intentional breaking of confidentiality by researchers is an action which is frowned on by the research community. However, it is recognised that there may be occasions when researchers might be obliged, or feel they need, to break confidentiality (see American Sociological Association, 1999; British Sociological Association, 2002; British Educational Research Association, 2004; British Psychological Society, 2009). Legal and regulatory frameworks influence how these issues are dealt with (Masson, 2004; Montgomery, 2002). This is particularly the case in some areas of research, such as in research with children and in health contexts. Regulatory frameworks, such as research governance procedures or ethical guidelines, may also influence the freedom researchers have to make decisions on these issues. Legal frameworks include Article 8 of the Human Rights Act 1998, the Children's Act 1989, 2004 and the Data Protection Act 1998 which have relevance to confidentiality in relation to research (Montgomery, 2002).

In general, researchers have a common law duty of confidentiality to research participants but there are certain circumstances which may override this duty, for example if there is an overriding duty to the public such as might occur in relation to a serious criminal offence or in life-threatening circumstances. In addition, researchers may feel a moral duty (although there is no legal *obligation*) to disclose information if a study participant reports being a victim of crime or if a researcher feels a study participant is at risk of harm. This issue is particularly pertinent, and has been widely debated, in relation to child abuse (Bostock, 2002); where researchers view a child or young person at risk of physical or psychological harm it would be expected that they would take some action to report it. Practitioner researchers, such as social workers and teachers, have a professional responsibility (a 'duty of care') to report situations or individuals they have concerns about to their managers or other professionals. They are at risk of disciplinary action if they do not do so (Masson, 2004; Allmark, 2002). There is, in addition, specific regulation in relation to the work of particular professionals and some groups (for example specific local authority child protection procedures in the UK as set out in the Children's Act 1989, 2004). Health professionals may also feel a 'duty of care' as part of their professional registration to inform others if they have concerns about individuals that are uncovered during research, for example those perceived to be at risk of serious ill health by not complying with a medical regimen. There are additionally some diseases that must, by law, be notified to public health authorities.

Situations in which promises of confidentiality might need to be breached should be minimised by researchers thinking through the circumstances in which they might feel they need to break confidentiality prior to approaching research participants. Study participants should be alerted to these as part of the consent process (Ritchie and Lewis 2003; Wright *et al*, 2004; the DVRG, 2004). This means that participants are made aware of the circumstances in which confidentiality cannot be maintained and leaves the decision with the participant whether or not they identify them. In identifying the issues that warrant breaking confidentiality, researchers need to consider participants' safety and well-being and also various legal, regulatory and professional frameworks to which they are subject. This involves giving careful consideration to the types of issues that might emerge in the context of a specific research project that a researcher might feel it is in the best interests of research participants to report to others and setting these out when they consent people to a study. This might involve, for example, saying to research participants 'everything you tell me will be kept confidential unless you tell me something about you or someone else being harmed or being at risk of harm. If this happens I will need to talk to you about what we should do about it'. Research ethics committees are likely to expect to see evidence that researchers have given careful consideration to these issues. However, a difficulty arises if issues emerge that researchers had not expected and had not alerted participants to as part of the consent process. The expectation is that, should unanticipated issues emerge during a study, the researcher should always discuss the need to disclose this and get participants' permission before doing so (Ritchie and Lewis 2003; Wright *et al*, 2004).

A problem arises for the researcher if the participant does not agree to the issue being disclosed and there is little discussion in the literature on how this should be managed. Most researchers appear to feel that unless a research participant gives permission for information about them to be disclosed then researchers should not do so (Wiles, Crow *et al*, 2008). The exception to this would be cases of people (especially minors) at risk of serious harm, although of course what constitutes 'serious harm' in different research contexts will be subject to varying interpretations. In such cases discussion of the issue with supervisors, peers or a research ethics committee prior to taking action is appropriate. If the decision to disclose information without the permission of the participant is made, it would be expected that participants are informed of this decision. It is clearly important that researchers are aware of what their legal responsibilities are and that they think through, and can justify, their moral duty to participants in such cases. One researcher participant taking part in our research study on informed consent noted:

> Well I think it's a bit of a grey area because the teachers have a duty to report [but] do researchers? I think we may not be covered by the letter of the law but I think in the spirit of the law we have to report. I think I would have to say to the child, the promise of confidentiality would have to be framed in terms of the fact that if I find they're in danger, then I would have to speak to somebody but I'd try and do it with them. (Wiles, Crow *et al*, 2008: 420)

Criminological research raises some specific issues in relation to confidentiality in that information about illegal or criminal activity might be identified in the process of the research. The identification of illegal activity, or activities on the boundaries of legality, such as drug taking, falsely claiming benefits, underage drinking or sexual activity might of course arise in any research project. The decision about whether or not illegal or immoral activity should be kept confidential may be a difficult one. Reporting of criminal activity identified through a research project inevitably risks alienating research participants and perhaps preventing subsequent research being conducted. In our research project on informed consent, we found that researchers do not feel obliged to report criminal or immoral activity, providing no one is at risk of physical harm (Wiles, Crow *et al*, 2008). Indeed in some research contexts concerning illegal activity, the fieldwork is conducted on the understanding that the information provided will be kept confidential. However, researchers need to be aware that they may be forced to breach confidentiality and provide information should the authorities become aware that they have it. The research literature indicates there have been no cases where social researchers have been forced to reveal information collected for research purposes in the UK although such cases have been reported in North America (Lee, 1993: 164; van den Hoonard, 2002: 8). This appears to be an area of great uncertainty for researchers which involves them having to balance issues of legality and morality in how they manage their research. Iphofen (2009: 101) sums this up in this way:

The prime dilemma is to balance the moral stance of confidentiality, with the legal position, while also judging the 'seriousness' of any reported offence and balancing that against the potential danger to 'as yet unknown' others who could be harmed by non-reporting.

Most researchers in the UK working in these areas appear to work in ways that enable them to avoid any legal pressure to divulge information. However, increasing levels of ethical regulation and concerns with risks to institutional reputation may present a challenge to these ways of working (see Adler and Adler, 2002). Researchers working in such areas should seek advice from their organisation's legal representative or research support office prior to conducting research.

Accidental disclosures

Accidental breaches of confidentiality can occur in a range of ways. Accidental disclosures can occur when researchers discuss their research with peers (or others), in the process of presenting research at conferences or other forums and in publications. It needs to be remembered that the anonymisation of individuals does not mean that they cannot be identified by others. Clark (see Wiles, Prosser *et al*, 2008: 30), for example, found that despite his best efforts at anonymisation, someone attending a presentation he gave was able to accurately identify the specific individual presented in a quote. In this specific case, the presence of visual clues about an anonymised place provided enough information to enable the participant to be identified:

> Despite our best efforts, we did not entirely resolve the challenges of anonymising place. In some instances a failure to anonymise place can also unwittingly reveal the identities of individual participants as well. For example, the use of a quotation positioned alongside a particular photograph (in this case, of a patch of waste-ground in my research site) during a seminar paper I gave was sufficient to enable one member of the audience who was familiar with the research site to identify the participant who gave the quotation, even though I believed I had anonymised both participant and name of the fieldsite and ensured there was, seemingly, no identifying feature in the photograph.

Particular difficulties with disclosure of confidentiality occur in research projects involving high profile and distinctive individuals, such as Government ministers or a CEO of a company. It may be impossible to anonymise such individuals, and not necessarily desirable to do so. Indeed it may be that individuals such as these choose to be identified and to speak 'on the record'. These individuals are likely to be clear about what they are willing and not willing to discuss in a research interview and the implications of doing so. For these individuals, concerns about confidentiality may be minimal.

Research involving individuals who have distinct roles and who choose to be anonymous, such as a head teacher of a school or hospital manager, may pose greater difficulties in relation to confidentiality, particularly when a study involves one or a small number of organisations or groups. In part the risks to confidentiality arise because, even though a research site and an individual may be anonymised, views expressed often need to be identified by a particular position (for example, head teacher) in various dissemination fora for the research to make sense. Confidentiality of individuals can often be easily breached by the inclusion of contextual information, such as a general location (for example 'a city on the South Coast of England' can be only a few places), a description of an organisation or some factual information about it. It is often easy to take an educated guess on the basis of descriptive information or to conduct a Google search that will identify, for example, the identity of a school on the basis of its Ofsted Report or the identity of a hospital on the basis of waiting times for specific surgical procedures. Once an organisation is identified, readers may feel they are able to guess at the identity of an individual's views set out in a report of the research. Although of course this may be only a guess on their part this will not necessarily prevent consequences flowing from it. Research with people who have distinct experiences which might enable them to be easily identified are another group for whom confidentiality issues are raised.

As well as considerations of confidentiality to the external world there are considerations of internal confidentiality to consider; that is, confidentiality of participants to other participants in the same organisation or group. Study participants within an organisation taking part in research are likely to know who else is taking part and may ask a researcher what their colleagues have said or indeed a manager may ask what their employees have said about particular issues. While it may be clear that such requests for information should not be met, a researcher may nevertheless inadvertently recount a seemingly innocuous event or comment to a participant that has arisen through the research that has unanticipated consequences for another participant. Additionally, participants within a specific organisation or group that are the subject of research are likely to be able to take an educated guess at people's identities within a research report and this can have unintended consequences. These issues of internal confidentiality are not necessarily confined to research taking place in organisations and may equally apply to research focusing on families or friendship networks. In research taking place in organisations or with networks of individuals, great care needs to be taken to ensure that confidentiality is maintained and that sensitive material is managed in ways that do not jeopardise individuals' well-being and their relationships with others. It has been noted that a number of harms might arise from confidentiality breaches which, depending on the context, may range from embarrassment to violence (Lee, 1993: 191). A researcher interviewed in our study on informed consent (Wiles, Crow *et al*, 2008: 424) noted in the context of research within families that a number of difficult issues arise in relation to this:

> There are really difficult issues when you are interviewing members of a family or couples, or people who are in a relationship and you are putting their accounts side by side. There are some very difficult issues there and we often try to side-step them by changing enough so that we're hoping that the person they're talking about won't be able to recognise themselves if they read it. It's very common for people to tell you things that you think would be hugely problematic if their relatives knew they'd said that ... I think it's important to exercise judgement about the impact that that could have in the network that the person comes from.

In situations where accidental disclosures of confidentiality might occur, various steps can be taken to limit disclosure (see Lee, 1993). In some cases it may be possible to write about particular findings in general ways, and to avoid the use of direct quotations, to limit the risk of identification. However, in other cases it may be necessary to omit some data, especially when data are particularly sensitive or when its inclusion could have negative consequences if the individual were identified. Sometimes it may be necessary to exclude individual cases altogether in order to protect people's identities, especially in cases where dramatic or extreme situations are described which are likely to make individuals identifiable. Another strategy is to change some aspect of the identity of an organisation or an individual in the description of a case or in the attribution given to various individuals when quotes are used. So, for example, an individual might be ascribed a different gender, job or medical condition in order to reduce the likelihood of their being identified. However, if such an approach is used, great care needs to be taken to ensure this doesn't affect the integrity of the data. Some researchers are very much against the idea of 'tampering' with data in this way and methods textbooks and research guidelines note the difficulties in balancing 'disguise and distortion' (Lee, 1993: 187; Becker and Bryman, 2004: 345; British Sociological Association, 2002: 4; Social Research Association, 2003: 39). Certainly such an approach needs careful consideration and justification. One researcher from our study on informed consent (Wiles, Crow *et al*, 2008: 423) noted:

> Some of the people I've interviewed have got very distinctive stories and you have to develop ways of ensuring their anonymity. [...] Sometimes when there's an issue that I want to get on the printed page but I need to preserve their anonymity then I might turn a him into a her or change the age or the part of the country. [...] You'd only do that if it doesn't make any difference to the message you're giving, and sometimes it does and sometimes it doesn't.

In situations where there are specific concerns about confidentiality, it is advisable to liaise closely with study participants about the ways in which data will be reported. This may involve sharing transcripts or other data (such as observational notes or photographs) with participants and getting consent for their use. In the case of transcripts this may involve inviting study participants to amend the transcript and agree to its use. It may also involve showing, and getting agreement for, the use of specific pieces of data (such as photographs or interview extracts) in outputs. Arguably, this is an approach that should always be adopted regardless of specific concerns about confidentiality. Certainly people's concerns about confidentiality and the limits of confidentiality that can be provided are influenced by the form of dissemination. A public viewing, community presentation or an article in a local paper or organisational newsletter are likely to raise more concerns for individuals about confidentiality than a presentation at an academic conference or a paper in an academic journal. Researchers are best placed to explain to study participants the risks involved in particular forms of dissemination to enable participants to make informed decisions about how their data are used.

'Off the record' comments

Another form of confidential data that researchers sometimes have to deal with is comments which study participants make during the course of research which they don't want included in the research. Such comments are often prefaced with 'I wouldn't want this included', 'I wouldn't want anyone to know about this' or 'this is off the record'. Sometimes a participant may ask for a recording device to be turned off while they make the comment but in other situations the comments may be recorded. Managing these sorts of comments can be difficult. Clearly once a researcher has been told something, albeit confidentially, they cannot be unaware of it. Indeed, study participants may want the researcher to know certain things so that the research is informed by these issues even though they do not want the comment to be ascribed to them personally. In general, comments made by individuals that they ask to be kept confidential cannot be used; it would be a breach of confidentiality to do so. However, it may be possible to negotiate with study participants the ways in which they would be willing for (and perhaps even want) the information they have provided to be used. Where a full transcript including the 'confidential' comments has been made, participants can be sent the transcript and asked if they would still like it excluded or whether they might be willing to reformulate the points in a way that would enable the information to form part of the research, if appropriate. Research exploring people's experiences of particular services, such as experiences of health care provision, can result in people complaining about poor levels of care. While they may not want to have their specific case identified, they may still want the research to reflect the concerns they have.

Anonymisation

The primary way that researchers seek to protect research participants from the accidental breaking of confidentiality is through the process of anonymisation, which occurs through the use of pseudonyms applied to research participants, organisations and locations. Anonymity of research participants is a central feature of ethical research practice which is written into the various guidelines to which social researchers work. Additionally, the Data Protection Act (1998) provides the legal framework for anonymisation of data. While complete anonymity may be difficult to achieve, it is recommended that all identifying data are removed prior to publication and, where an individual may be identifiable, explicit consent must be obtained before publication can proceed.

Pseudonyms are generally chosen by the researcher, but are sometimes given by a transcriber or suggested by participants. The use of pseudonyms is not without its problems in relation to successful anonymisation. Iphofen (2009: 94) notes that selecting pseudonyms that appear well-suited to the characteristics of a participant can pose confidentiality risks in that they may 'offer subtle or latent clues' to an individual's identity. Grinyer (2002), however, notes that using pseudonyms that are not 'equivalent' in some way to a participant's real name can seem inappropriate. Names can have specific social class, age and ethnic connotations and, arguably, their use can distort the meaning attributed to quotations. Providing people with the opportunity to choose their own pseudonym can also pose problems; Corden and Sainsbury (2006) note that researchers have found that participants sometimes choose the names of real people, such as their friends and Grinyer (2002) notes the difficulty of managing the situation if more than one participant wishes to choose the same pseudonym.

Pseudonyms are often given to locations; however, the descriptions and/or images provided, as noted above, make it relatively easy to identify, or at least make an educated guess, where a study is located (Clark, 2006). There are considerable examples of community research where people have been unhappy about the way they or their community has been characterised and of the ramifications this has had (see Crow and Wiles, 2008). This indicates a need to consider issues of anonymity and consent in relation to place as carefully as to people.

Identification

Some researchers have questioned the assumption that participants always want to be anonymised. There has been a growing trend to recognising that research participants often want to be identified in research outputs and that, in much social research, there is no good reason not to allow that to happen (Tilley and Woodthorpe, 2011). Anne

Grinyer's (2002) important paper on this topic describes her experience conducting research with parents of young adults with cancer in which she sought her research participants' views about the anonymisation of their accounts and the use of pseudonyms. Grinyer found that three quarters of her respondents wanted to have their own names used in the research rather than a pseudonym and, as a result, a mix of real names and pseudonyms were used in publications, reflecting participants' wishes. Researchers conducting research with children and young people as well as the bereaved have found that research participants often want their own names and/or the names of their deceased relatives to be used (see Wiles *et al*, 2011). In a study of research participants' views of the use of verbatim quotations in qualitative research, Corden and Sainsbury (2006) also found that research participants did not like the use of pseudonyms. Grinyer (2002: 4) notes the importance of providing research participants the opportunity to use their own names but notes that this must be balanced with protecting them from harm:

> The balance of protecting respondents from harm by hiding their identity while at the same time preventing 'loss of ownership' is an issue that needs to be addressed by each researcher on an individual basis with each respondent.

A further difficulty arises in research being conducted within a specific group, network or organisation in which some people opt for identification but others do not. The identification of some individuals can lead to the identification of others who wish to remain anonymous. In this situation, identification cannot be offered without breaching confidentiality for others. A similar situation occurs in relation to an organisation; in cases where an institution wants to remain anonymous it may not be possible to enable participants to opt for identification, at least not without the consent of the institution. One of our participants in our study on informed consent noted (Wiles, Crow *et al*, 2008: 425):

> One of the intensive care units was bitterly disappointed that her unit wasn't named, but I had to explain that if I identified the unit then there would be a cascade of identification, you know, and people would be able to potentially identify all the staff and all the patients.

Visual data and anonymisation

Visual research, particularly where photographs and film are used as data, presents particular challenges for anonymity. Much of this type of visual material makes the anonymisation of individuals or locations problematic if not impossible (Clark, 2006; Wiles, Prosser *et al*, 2008; Wiles, Clark and Prosser, 2011). Challenges to anonymity may also arise with other forms of visual data, such as drawings and collage (see Prosser and Loxley 2008; Wiles *et al*, 2011). The situation is complicated by the fact that individuals appear commonly to want to be identified in their visual images, a similar situation to that which emerges in some text-based research as discussed above.

Still and moving visual images that portray clearly identifiable individuals can be anonymised only by altering the image in some way so as to obscure an individual's identity. More commonly, visual researchers present these types of visual material in their entirety, thereby enabling individuals to be identified, with their consent (see Pink, 2007). Methods of obscuring people's identity include increasing the pixilation of facial features in order to blur them, the use of specific anonymisation software that converts visual images into drawn images and blocking out eyes, faces or other distinguishing features (see Wiles, Prosser *et al*, 2008). Obscuring facial features alone may not be adequate to ensure anonymity in that there may be a range of other visual clues in the image that enable an individual to be identified. Obscuring facial features has been subject to criticism by some social researchers (Williams *et al* (undated): 7; Sweetman, 2008). Nevertheless, it is recognised that there are some individuals, groups or types of images that necessitate the identities of individuals being obscured. It is common practice, for example, for researchers working with children to use specialist software to anonymise children's images (Flewitt, 2005; Wiles, Prosser *et al*, 2008).

The more common approach favoured by many social researchers is to present visual data in their entirety, with consent, and not to attempt to anonymise individuals (see for example, Back, 2004; Holliday, 2004). In this mode of working, pseudonyms are not generally used. Many researchers who work with visual material have identified the importance of developing relationships of mutual trust with study participants so that the images that are taken emerge from collaborations between researcher and study participant and are jointly owned (Banks, 2001; Gold, 1989;

Harper, 1998; Pink, 2007). This involves showing images to participants, and allowing them to comment on them, prior to publication or presentation, as well as consideration by researchers of the political, social and cultural contexts in which images will be viewed and interpreted. There may however be a tension between study participants' wishes about how images of them are used and researchers' responsibility to protect them from harm. Collaboration with research participants on issues around anonymity and dissemination involve more than simply meeting participants' wishes; researchers need to consider carefully and explain the various implications to individuals and in some cases it may be necessary to override their wishes if this is viewed as being in study participants' best interests.

The longevity of visual and other data which can remain in the public domain through publication in books and articles for many years, if not indefinitely, also raises some issues that warrant consideration with research participants. While an individual may be happy for a specific image or expressed view to be made public at one point in their lives they may be less so in the future as their circumstances change, yet once something enters the public domain it may be difficult or impossible to remove it. The internet offers considerable opportunities for global dissemination but, without restricted access to sites, raises the possibilities that data can be copied and reproduced in contexts other than those for which they were obtained. This also raises specific issues in relation to the storage and archiving of research data. There is a need to ensure that all data are stored in ways that ensure confidentiality and that express consent is provided for their continued and subsequent use.

Summary

Confidentiality and anonymity are distinct but related concepts; confidentiality refers to the need to keep identifiable information about individuals private and anonymity is one of the ways in which data are kept confidential. Intentional disclosure of information may be necessary in certain circumstances if research participants are viewed as being at risk. Accidental disclosures of information also occur but care should be taken to avoid these where possible. There is an increasing trend in research towards research participants being identified rather than anonymised.

5 Risk and safety

Introduction

Ensuring the safety and well-being of research participants is an important element of ethical research practice. While much qualitative research may pose only minimal risks to participants it is important not to disregard the risks that can occur, particularly in research on topics which are in some way 'sensitive' because they focus on personal issues, taboo issues or issues which pose a threat for those participating in it (see Lee, 1993). Such research also poses significant risks for researchers which should not be overlooked. Consideration should also be given to wider risks to researchers' institutions, their disciplines and the field of study.

Risks for research participants

All activities pose some level of risk and research participation is no exception. It is generally accepted that participation in research should pose no more than minimal risk to participants, that researchers should assess the potential risks and that participants should be fully informed of these as well as the benefits of taking part in research. In response to the increased ethical regulation of social research, various authors have noted that the risks of harm arising from social research are minimal at most, if not non-existent (see, for example, Atkinson, 2009; Dingwall, 2008). Certainly, in comparison with medical research the risks from social research are slight. However, this does not mean that risk of harm does not exist and authors such as Kent *et al* (2002) and van Teijlingen (2006) have disputed the assumption that social research is risk-free.

Assessing risk of harm

Assessing risks that might arise as a result of taking part in a research project involves researchers reflecting on the nature of risk and harm and the ways in which their research might present risks to participants' well-being. Assessments of risk involve considerations of the potential for harm, both physical and psychological or emotional, as well as practical issues such as the costs participants might incur as a result of participating in research in terms of money, time and inconvenience. The range of risks that need consideration is discussed below.

The potential benefits of research also need to be considered, both to the research participants themselves and to the community or society more widely, so that research participants and researchers can assess whether the potential risks outweigh the benefits. Balancing possible risks of harm and the potential for benefit is far from straightforward. Risks of harm are generally (but not always) experienced by an individual but benefits are often to groups, communities or society more generally. It is also the case that benefits arising from research, such as a change in policy or provision for a specific group, are often long term and, if they occur at all, may do so some time after the research project has been completed. The Research Ethics Guidebook (http://www.ethicsguidebook.ac.uk/) makes the important point that benefits need to be thought of, and articulated to participants as, 'hoped for' outcomes of research rather than those that are guaranteed, noting that this terminology is 'more honest about the uncertainty underlying all research'. Researchers may, for example, hope that their research brings about a change in the way groups are perceived, or the treatment or provision they receive, but these hoped-for benefits may not occur as a result of one specific research project; indeed it may have no impact on the individual participant's experiences. It is certainly important not to raise participants' expectations about what the outcomes of the research may be.

Individuals may experience personal benefits as a result of taking part in research, such as feeling listened to, having an opportunity to express their views or feeling that their views will influence policy or practice. Some researchers have reported that their participants have gained considerable benefits as a result of being able to talk about issues or experiences with an independent person that they haven't been able to discuss with anyone else. However, it cannot be assumed that such benefits will occur. It is not the purpose of research to bring about such benefits; if they occur they are perhaps best seen as a side effect of research participation.

Clearly, if risks to participants are greater than minimal and the benefits not evident then there is little justification for the research being conducted. However, who should make that decision? Arguably, participants are best placed to make decisions about the risks they are willing to take in relation to participating in research. Researchers, or indeed research ethics committees, who decide on participants' behalf that a project or method is too risky for participants have been accused of paternalism (Hope, 2004, Pels, 2008). Nevertheless, researchers often experience a conflict between seeking to protect study participants on the one hand but allowing them the agency to make decisions about the risks they are willing to take on the other (Wiles *et al*, 2011).

Assessments of risk, harm and benefit are far from straightforward. It is not possible to identify all risks that an individual might encounter from participating in research. A researcher cannot know what an individual might find distressing and even fairly innocuous research topics can result in a research participant becoming distressed. In a study on private health care that I undertook many years ago, one of the first interviews I undertook focused on a man's hospital stay for a minor routine operation and resulted in him crying as he recalled his wife's serious illness twenty years previously. I could not have predicted this response and neither could the interviewee when he agreed to participate. Similarly, Jaimie Ellis, a PhD student, found that what she thought was an activity that was likely to pose little risk to the autistic teenagers taking part in her research resulted in considerable distress for one young person. In her research, the participants were asked to write an essay about their imagined future:

> The class started with a discussion each taking it in turns to talk about what they might do as adults. Mrs Morrsion [the teacher] asked the class where they might be living when they are older. Vishal responded with a definite "16. House of my own". The same question was asked of Ben ... Ben burst into a flood of tears. "No, no I don't want to live on my own, I'm just a teenager". We were all a little surprised by the tears. "Will you leave home when you're older Ben?" asked Mrs Morrison. Ben [said] "No, no I want to stay at school, I'm just a teenager". He seemed to have forgotten or misunderstood that the task was about the future and not the present. He threw his head into his hands in a panic ... and flopped down on the table sobbing into his arm. (Ellis, 2011, field notes)

Both of these examples illustrate the importance of emergent ethics, of thinking about, and managing, ethical issues and risk throughout the lifetime of a research project. The important point to note is that while it is important that researchers think carefully about potential risks and benefits of participating in research and inform participants so that they can decide whether or not they want to take part, neither researchers not participants necessarily know what issues might emerge in the process of the research and how they will be responded to by participants.

Types of risk

A range of potential risks of taking part in qualitative research have been identified. Most risks of social research relate to participants' psychological or emotional well-being. Risks to participants' physical well-being are less likely but not unheard of (see Lee, 1993). Risks to well-being have been identified as arising from: an emotional response during data collection; an emotional response to ending involvement with a project; and the effect of the publication of research findings.

Perhaps the most common type of risk arises from a participant's response to a question asked or topic discussed during fieldwork. People becoming upset or distressed is probably a relatively common experience in qualitative research, particularly in research on so called 'sensitive' topics (Lee, 1993). However, research can also engender other emotional responses in response to researchers' questions or activities. Embarrassment, humiliation or anxiety can occur in response to insensitive questions, questions or tasks that the research participant feels unable to answer or do, or topics or tasks that explore participants' underlying fears (see, for example, Grinyer, 2001). Research participants can feel deceived if they were not, or feel that they were not, told the 'real' reasons for undertaking the research. They may also feel devalued if they feel their views are disregarded or not taken seriously.

It has been observed that research participants can feel used by researchers and that they may feel disregarded or devalued as a result of participating in research. Researchers sometimes do engage in various activities to 'manipulate' participants to participate in research and to provide rich data, a process referred to by Bengry-Howell and Griffin (2011) as 'methodological grooming'. Such activities may leave participants feeling used after the research is completed and the researcher has exited from their lives, particularly if their expectations of benefits are not met. This is particularly the case with longitudinal research when participants build up relationships with researchers over prolonged periods. As Iphofen (2009: 53) notes:

> In longer term encounters ... the subject may need some 'closure' time and some opportunity to come to terms with a relationship that appeared to have friendship at its core but was, in effect, highly instrumental.

Considerable risks to participants can arise from the publication and dissemination of research; many of these issues have been discussed in chapter 4 on anonymity and confidentiality. Despite anonymisation, people may be upset at how they are portrayed in research reports. Crow and Wiles' (2008) review of community studies identified cases where some local residents were deeply unhappy about how they had been portrayed in publications. Such studies may also bring unwanted publicity, and media attention, to a research site given that the anonymisation of specific communities is notoriously difficult. The risk of unwanted media attention is not a risk only in community studies; it may also occur in research on specific groups or institutions or indeed in relation to categories of individuals. Research may result in negative publicity, and the reinforcement of stereotypes, about specific groups such as benefit claimants, young people, homeless people or ethnic minorities. The increasing pressure on researchers to provide evidence of the impact of their research and to get their research findings into the public domain may fuel these sorts of problems given the difficulties that researchers face in controlling how the media report their research findings.

Publication may also pose other risks where an individual's identity is disclosed, such as censure from others which might in some cases result in loss of friendship or employment. In research on political activity or illegal activity more extreme risks, including risk of physical harm or legal sanctions, might be present (see Lee, 1993).

Other risks concern the costs incurred, both financial and personal, from participating in research. These issues are often overlooked but warrant consideration. Such costs might be a loss of earnings incurred by taking time out to participate in research. Participants might also experience inconvenience; the time spent in participating in a project means they have less time to do other things they might want or need to do. Some of these factors can be offset, to some degree, by offering payments to participants in recognition of their contribution.

Minimising risks of harm

A number of ways have been identified to minimise and manage risks of harm from participating in research. Careful thought needs to be given prior to a study commencing of the possible risks of harm that the research might pose to individuals and/or the communities of which they are part. Research participants should have the risks and benefits of research participation explained to them as part of the consent process and make their own decisions about whether or not they want to participate. As discussed above, risks or harm should also be assessed throughout a research project as they emerge; the publication and dissemination of research are particular points when considerations of risks of harm need to be addressed. Research participants should also be informed, as part of the consent process, about who they can contact should they have a complaint about any aspect of their involvement in a study. Such complaints need to be reviewed and the research changed to take into account complaints as appropriate.

Strategies also need to be in place to manage any distress or discomfort that participants may experience during fieldwork. Research on a wide range of topics can generate emotional responses and researchers need to be sensitive to research participants' feelings. This may mean monitoring participants' body language for signs of fatigue or distress and responding to such signs by suggesting that data collection be suspended or stopped. It may also mean enabling people to decline to answer particular questions or discuss specific issues. For some groups, such as children or people in institutional settings, active encouragement for them to refuse to discuss particular issues may be necessary. In our research project on informed consent, researchers working with children reported providing participants with red cards that they could hold up if they didn't want to answer a particular question or didn't want to continue with the interview. They also noted the importance of researchers spending time with participants prior to the research commencing to enable them to 'rehearse' this so that they felt confident enough to do it. Another strategy identified was training participants to say 'pass' if they did not want to discuss specific topics (Wiles *et al*, 2005).

Involvement in research should mean that participants leave the research process feeling no more unhappy or distressed than they did when they began it. Of course it is not always in a researcher's power to ensure this is the case but debriefing after an interview or other data collection activity is an important means of researchers assessing participants' response to the research. It is often appropriate to provide information or resources about support that people can access if the research has, or might, raise issues that an individual finds distressing. Such support might, for example, be contact numbers for the Citizens Advice Bureau, a counselling service or support groups relevant to the topic of the research.

Risks to researchers

Managing risks to researchers throughout a research project is an important, and often neglected, consideration. Bloor *et al*'s (2007) inquiry into the risk to well-being of researchers in qualitative research provides an extremely useful exploration of the issues. They note that:

> While research-related harm thankfully remains comparatively rare, the evidence ... suggests that it is a more common phenomenon than the absence of formal complaints would suggest. (Bloor *et al*, 2007: 5)

There are two types of potential risks to researchers, physical risks and emotional risks, with the latter seeming to be the more common.

Physical risks

'Physical' risks comprise actual physical harm or threat of physical harm. Bloor *et al* (2007) note that cases of serious injury and death are rare in social research and that fear of harm is greater than actual cases of injury. Nevertheless, some deaths of researchers have been reported (Bloor *et al*, 2007: 18) and, as Kenyon and Hawker (1999) note, 'once would be enough', in other words, the fact that it is rare is little consolation if you are the rare case who experiences physical harm. While it is important not to overstate the risks, it is crucial that researchers carefully assess what potential risks might arise and make attempts to minimise them. Risks of physical harm arise from three aspects of a research project: the location, the topic and the participants, all of which may be interlinked.

In terms of location, risk of physical harm can occur when conducting research in some locations or settings. Considerations of physical harm generally focus on risks from others 'in the field'. However, the risk of illness and disease, particularly when working in developing countries, should not be overlooked. Lee's (1995) distinction between 'ambient' and 'situational' danger is a useful one when considering physical risks to researchers; ambient danger refers to research conducted in dangerous environments or locations and situational danger refers to risks arising from the presence of a researcher in a setting which may provoke aggression or hostility from members of the group being researched (Lee, 1993: 10; Lee, 1995: 3). In many cases both ambient and situational dangers may be present. Ambient danger is present in volatile research environments or settings, such as research conducted in war zones or areas in which there is political or social unrest. Risks may arise simply by being in a dangerous environment and the everyday risks of such an environment (such as being injured by gunfire or in an anti-Government demonstration). Dangers may also exist when conducting research in unfamiliar settings and cultures which do not, on the face of it, present obvious dangers, particularly when research-ers are working overseas. Such dangers may arise from not understanding safe ways of conducting oneself in a different culture, such as the areas in which it is safe for a woman to walk alone at night. They may also arise from reacting to cultural practices which a researcher deems as disturb-ing. Iphofen (2009: 86) notes that researchers can expose themselves to physical danger if they record or try to intervene in particular occurrences, such as the mistreatment of individuals. These risks are not confined to research being conducted in countries with which the researcher is not familiar. Similar risks also occur in researching various subcultures in a researcher's 'home' country. It has been noted that it is anthropological fieldwork (and perhaps also ethnography) that poses the greatest dangers to researchers in terms of physical harm (Iphofen, 2009: 86).

The risks associated with particular topics are closely linked with the location of research. Research focusing on activities defined as illegal or deviant in some way, such as drug use, football hooliganism and a range of criminal activities, may raise a number of risks of physical harm to researchers. Risk of harm may come from members of the group being studied who take a dislike to the focus of the research or the questions asked by the researcher or it may come from people who are external to the group who pose a threat to the group as a whole, which may include the researcher. Risk of physical harm is greater in covert research with such groups and may result if the researcher's true identity is disclosed. Physical harm is also a risk if participant observer roles are adopted to such an extent that the researcher 'goes native' and takes on the identity of the group being studied. In such cases the researcher may find themselves embroiled in activities that place them in physical danger. Other types of topics that may engender risk of physical harm for researchers who adopt some form of participative ethnographic approach are those that focus on 'dangerous' recreational activities, such as speedway or rally driving, or types of employment, such as roofers or security 'bouncers' (see Bloor *et al*, 2007: 19). Here the physical risk is not necessarily from research participants but from the activity itself. Griffin and Bengry-Howell (2008), for example, in an ethnographic study of young working-class men who modify their cars, reflect on the decision taken by Bengry-Howell to have a ride in the car of one of the study participants:

> [He] willingly put his life at risk in pursuance of research goals, by getting into a car that belonged to a person he vaguely knew who had admitted during interview that he had a penchant for driving at high speeds. On the other hand, the opportunity to actually sit alongside Jonno in his car, whilst he demonstrated what his car could do, had enabled [him] ... to directly experience the way in which the cultural practice of driving at high speeds operated within the context of the car modifier's world. (Griffin and Bengry-Howell, 2008: 28)

Individuals can pose risks to researchers in the contexts and ways outlined above but there are potentially additional risks that an individual may pose to a researcher's physical well-being unrelated to the geographical location or topic of the research. The context of much qualitative research involves researchers collecting data with individuals in private places, often study participants' homes. This often involves interviewing individuals that are unknown to them. The risk of the lone researcher coming into contact with someone who poses a physical threat to them is unlikely but nevertheless possible and it appears to be something about which researchers experience great unease (Kenyon and Hawker, 1999). It is certainly the case that being alone in a stranger's home does place researchers in a potentially vulnerable situation. Participants in Kenyon and Hawker's (1999) study report cases of serious harm and considerable anxiety about the potential for such harm. This issue is one which organisations have taken seriously as part of risk assessment procedures. There are several strategies which researchers can, and should, adopt to maximise their safety.

Organisations that employ researchers, and support research students, have a responsibility to protect them from harm. However, while there are generally formal structures in place, such as risk assessment procedures, insurance and lone working policies, these do not appear to be universally used by those who manage research and, in some cases, may offer inadequate safeguards even where they are used (Bloor *et al*, 2007: 4). Various recommendations, guidelines and protocols aimed at maintaining researchers' physical safety have been made (Bloor *et al*, 2007; Kenyon and Hawker, 1999; McCosker *et al*, 2001; Social Research Association, 2001). These include making careful assessments of risk in relation to the physical location of the fieldwork site, such as whether there are local tensions, political unrest or general safety issues for an individual in being located in and moving around the area. Assessments of risk in relation to data collection are also necessary and care is advised particularly in relation to individual interviews conducted in private places. Protocols for managing safety in such contexts, including leaving details of the interview location with a colleague with a plan for action if the researcher does not return at the expected time, are important. In some contexts it may be that it is more appropriate to use pairs of researchers to conduct interviews or to arrange interviews in public places. The Social Research Association's Code of Practice on Safety (2001) provides comprehensive advice on a range of issues relating to researcher safety (see also Iphofen, 2009: 88).

Emotional risks

The greater risk to researchers in undertaking qualitative research has been identified to be to their emotional well-being. This can include emotional trauma and, more commonly, emotional distress. Qualitative research generally necessitates researchers empathising with their participants in the process of collecting data. In much research, particularly research on 'sensitive' topics such as sexual abuse, suicide, terminal illness, bereavement and family breakdown, this involves researchers listening to people's experiences of hardship, grief, loss or fear. Such research can leave researchers feeling emotionally distressed and there is considerable evidence that this is widespread among qualitative researchers (Bloor *et al*, 2007: 44). Bloor *et al* (2007) describe research on emotionally demanding topics as a form of what Hochschild (1983) has termed 'emotional labour' in that researchers have to manage their emotions in the process of hearing about or observing the emotions, feelings and experiences of their research participants in the interest of obtaining 'good data' and managing the research process. Watts (2008) describes the feelings generated in her ethnographic study of a cancer drop-in centre:

> The emotion that has dominated participants' narratives in this study is fear ... the seeking of reassurance is emotionally distressing because whatever response I give, it will not be the one they covet, which is the promise of cure and the certainty of a longer life. Whilst they continue to hope I am sometimes laid low in my spirit. (Watts, 2008: 7)

Of course some researchers view it as important to engage emotionally with their research participants and to 'give something back' to them not only by revealing information about themselves and their experiences but by developing longer-term relationships with them (Oakley, 1981). However, this does not necessarily protect them from experiencing emotional distress and indeed may result in increased levels of distress as well as raising ethical dilemmas inherent in maintaining what may in effect be unequal relationships. In the face of emotional distress, a desire to help research participants is often provoked by observing or hearing about distressing events or experiences in the process of fieldwork. Brannen (1988) notes that such a response may have more to do with helping the researcher come to terms with the emotions evoked by the interview rather than helping the respondent (see Lee, 1993: 106). Adopting a position of 'proxy counsellor' or 'emotional helper' to research participants is certainly replete with problems; researchers do not necessarily have the skills to manage their respondents' emotional responses and it is, arguably, unethical to adopt such a role (Bloor *et al*, 2007: 26; Watts, 2008).

Emotional trauma can result from distressing memories on the part of the researcher being generated by the research. Emotional difficulties can also result from the process of observing practices or hearing about experiences or views to which a researcher is morally opposed but to which they are obliged to 'go along with' in order to avoid jeopardising the research. Other emotional difficulties that researchers have reported while in the field are feelings of isolation and lack of support. This is a particular issue for PhD students who, despite supervision, tend to work alone while in the field. It is also an issue for researchers working overseas in unfamiliar surroundings, a particular issue for many anthropologists.

A number of strategies have been identified to manage risks of emotional distress arising from the research process. Good preparation prior to entering the field is obviously important, and often overlooked (see Johnson and Macleod Clark, 2003). Placing limits on the amount of time spent in the field and/or interspersing data collection with time spent with other members of the research team or with research supervisors is one important management strategy. Counselling from a professional counsellor independent of the research team has been identified as potentially useful if specific problems occur, although this does not appear to be a widely-used strategy (see Corden *et al*, 2005). Most useful, and commonly used, appears to be a range of self-care strategies including opportunities for debriefing in research teams or with peers and using such groups as a source of support (Corden *et al*, 2005; Watts, 2008). Where procedures for debriefing are not set up as part of a research project, researchers may turn to informal support networks to 'offload' but this can raise issues of data confidentiality if clear understandings of confidentiality are not established as part of the process (Wiles, Crow *et al*, 2008). The use of a reflective diary or journal has been identified as another strategy for managing emotional distress (Bloor *et al*, 2007: 35).

Other risks

Other risks that researchers might encounter are reputational risks, to themselves as individuals, to their discipline and/or to their institution. Research governance procedures are likely to be in place in most institutions where researchers work to assess these risks prior to a study commencing, although problems may of course arise throughout a research project. Particular issues may arise in the process of publication of a study, particularly through engagement with the media. A degree of conflation, distortion and misinformation can occur which can have negative consequences for researchers and their institutions as well as their research participants. A website on research ethics produced by Lancaster University in the UK provides useful information on working with journalists (http://www.lancs.ac.uk/researchethics/8-1-mediapub. html#pressoffices). Reputational risk is also a factor in data archiving in that researchers form part of the data archived and feature in transcripts, field notes and detailed information about study design, data collection and analysis. The availability and scrutiny of these data by researchers for the purposes of secondary analysis may have particular reputational implications for early career researchers (see Neale and Bishop, 2012b). This issue is explored further in chapter 7.

Summary

Despite some researchers' claims that social research is relatively risk-free, there is evidence that it poses a range of potential risks for both research participants and researchers. The greatest risk in social research is to researchers' and their participants' emotional and psychological well-being. Consideration also needs to be given to the risks of lone working for researchers.

6 Ethical dilemmas

Introduction

This chapter outlines some of the everyday ethical dilemmas that researchers experience in the conduct of research. All research generates ethical issues of one type or another. Some of these can be predicted before the research commences but many have to be managed 'in the field' as the research proceeds. The dilemmas that emerge and the way that they are managed are inevitably specific to the research context and the researcher's moral and ethical framework. While there have been some ethical 'horror stories' in the social sciences, these are few and far between. For the most part, researchers manage the ethical issues that emerge in considered and reflexive ways that enable them to conduct research which will produce valid findings while at the same time treating research participants with respect. The need for careful consideration, evaluation and justification of ethical decisions is central to good ethical decision making.

Ethical 'horror stories'

There are some celebrated ethical 'horror stories' in the social sciences. The most commonly cited ones are two psychology experiments, Milgram's obedience to authority experiments which began in 1961 and Zimbardo's Stanford prison experiment conducted in 1971. Milgram's experiment involved research participants in the role of 'teacher' being told to administer what they thought was an electric shock to another person in the role of 'learner' if they failed a word test. Study participants continued to administer what they thought were electric shocks when told to do so, despite the apparent distress experienced by those receiving the shocks. Study participants were debriefed at the end of the experiment to explain the nature of the experiment and that the electric shocks were not real.

However, concerns have been raised about the anxiety generated among participants. Zimbardo's experiment was a study of the psychological effects of being a prisoner or prison guard. Students were allocated the role of 'prisoner' or 'prison guard' in a simulated prison. The experiment was stopped after six days due to the abusive behaviour of the 'guards' and the stress and anxiety experienced by the 'prisoners'. These two studies were behavioural experiments rather than qualitative studies.

A less commonly cited 'horror story' and one that is clearly qualitative is Laud Humphreys' ethnographic study of homosexuality conducted in 1970. Humphreys studied homosexual activity in public toilets in the park of a large US city. Humphreys acted as a 'lookout' in the toilets in order to observe the activity of the men. Most of this research was conducted covertly as he argued this was the only way this study could be conducted. In order to collect demographic information on the men he observed, Humphreys traced their home addresses via their car licence plates. He then approached them at home, disguised as a researcher conducting research on men's health, and asked them questions which enabled him to collect data on their race, marital status and occupation. Humphreys' study has been widely criticised as being unethical in virtually all aspects: his study involved deceit of participants both in the initial observation and follow-up interviews and he violated privacy. Nevertheless, the findings of the study did generate important insights and Humphreys has argued, from a consequentialist position, that this justifies the research design (see Warwick, 1982).

These 'ethical horror stories' in which problematic practice is central to the research design are relatively few and far between in qualitative research in the social sciences. While a number of horror stories have emerged from medical and experimental research, there appear to be far fewer in the social sciences, perhaps reflecting the much lower risks that qualitative social research poses for study participants. This of course does not mean that serious ethical breaches do not continue to occur in qualitative social research; it may be that we just do not get to hear about them. However, more likely is that there are very few cases of serious 'breaches', particularly in the current climate of ethical regulation of research. For the most part, the ethical issues that researchers encounter are managed carefully and reflexively and ethical horror stories are avoided. However, this does not mean that researchers do not experience ethical challenges and dilemmas in the process of conducting their research.

Below are some ethical dilemmas based on experiences reported by researchers. Rather than outlining how these ethical challenges were resolved these are presented as illustrations of the types of ethical challenges that emerge in research and as prompts for readers to reflect on ethical challenges.

Dilemma 1: In a study exploring people's experiences of recovery from a heart attack, an interviewee expressed extreme feelings of worthlessness resulting from his health condition which meant he was unable to work or to undertake activities he viewed as part of his male identity. Feeling he might be depressed and at risk, the interviewer suggested that he talked to his doctor about his feelings but he said he didn't want to do that as all the doctor would do would be to give him more medication. He also commented that he didn't want his wife to know or she would worry. The researcher promised confidentiality but was concerned about his mental health. Should she tell someone about him and if so, who?

Dilemma 2: In a study in an educational context exploring school-based friendships and using participatory and child-friendly research methods, the process for consent for children to participate in the study was that consent was needed from both the child and his/her parents. On the day the research was to take place, one child gave in her consent form on which the parent's signature had clearly been forged. The child denied they had forged it, and was desperate to take part in the research project and expressed anxiety about feeling excluded if she was unable to participate. Should the researcher overlook the forged consent given the research does not pose any risks to the child and indeed excluding them might be judged as more harmful?

Dilemma 3: A physiotherapist who is undertaking an ethnographic case-study project in a school for children with special needs for her PhD observed that a teaching assistant was encouraging a child to write rather than use a computer. The physiotherapist was aware that the child's physical condition was such that they will not have the dexterity to use a pen long-term and will need to develop computing skills in order to keep up with their work. However, her role in the school as a researcher who is observing interaction meant that if she intervened, the staff and the child would see her in a different light and this would be likely to impact on the relationships she had with them and the quality of data collected. However, if she did not intervene then she would not be acting in the best interests of the child which she was professionally obliged to do. Should she intervene in the interests of the child's well-being even if that does pose a risk to the research or should she continue to observe what is happening in the setting without affecting it?

These three dilemmas encompass the common broad ethical issues that researchers encounter in their research; issues of consent, anonymity, confidentiality, risk and role conflict. While these broad issues are common themes that emerge in research, the specific ethical dilemmas researchers experience within them are inevitably unique to the research project being undertaken. Consequently the way that dilemmas are managed is, to some degree, unique in that it must be the most appropriate decision in the light of the research topic, the participants and the context. As has been noted in chapter 2, ethical frameworks are important in helping research-ers to address ethical dilemmas but these do not provide an immediate answer. Rather, each issue must be carefully considered, drawing on ethical frameworks, in order to decide how it can be resolved.

Three detailed case studies are now presented. These draw on accounts of research in which ethical issues are described in some detail. They provide an exploration of three different types of dilemmas and how they were resolved in the context of the specific research project. These explore dilemmas of consent (Lawton, 2001), dilemmas of disclosure (Rowe, 2007) and dilemmas of confidentiality (Edwards and Weller, 2009).

case study

Dilemmas of consent: Julia Lawton

Julia Lawton's (2001) research was conducted in an in-patient hospice in the UK and explored the experiences of dying patients. The study aimed to explore the phenomenon of social death, that is the loss of identity and personhood that has been identified as occurring during the course of terminal illness, and the effects of a patient's death on other patients. Research in palliative care had, at the time the study was conducted, largely excluded dying people from research because of their assumed vulnerability and the considerable ethical and practical considerations such research raises. Lawton sought to address these concerns by conducting a participant observation approach in which she took on the role of an in-patient volunteer in order to unobtrusively observe patients and day-to-day life, and death, in the hospice. This observation was conducted with consent both from the hospice staff and patients. Patients were informed about the study by senior medical staff at the time that they were admitted to the hospice and were given the opportunity to opt out of any observations that were made. Despite the plans in place to manage the informed consent of hospice patients, several dilemmas in relation to consent were raised. A full discussion of the issues discussed here can be found in Lawton (2001).

The first dilemma concerned the difficulties in the process of gaining informed consent among a very fluid and ever-changing population. Large numbers of patients were admitted to the hospice and on some occasions, several patients were admitted at the same time in situations that were often chaotic because of patients' competing needs or the nature of an individual's medical condition. The admission of patients to the hospice was not necessarily a situation in which gaining informed consent for a study was a primary concern. As Lawton (2001: 698) notes:

> A fairly significant proportion of patients was admitted on an emergency basis ... it was not unusual for patients to be admitted in a state of extreme anxiety, experiencing very distressing symptoms, the consequences being that some were in no state to be informed of, let alone take in, the details of the research. A small proportion actually reached the hospice in a coma and died within a matter of hours of their admission.

So this first set of dilemmas about informed consent concerned whether it was always possible to assume that informed consent had been achieved prior to observation taking place. In such a busy and stressful environment patients clearly were not able to give lengthy consideration to whether or not they were willing to participate in a research project. It may also have been the case that not all patients would remember consenting to the study. The difficulty also emerged in relation to people who were comatose when they were admitted. In these cases, their family members were consulted for consent on their behalf but this raises a number of ethical dilemmas concerning whether or not relatives should be able to give consent for another person.

The second set of dilemmas concerned issues of ongoing consent. Consent was obtained at the time of admission to the hospice but this did not necessarily mean that patients remembered that the research was taking place in subsequent encounters with the researcher. This is a particularly problematic issue in participant observation. In this case, Lawton's role as a volunteer could have meant that patients viewed her primarily in this role rather than as a researcher. This led her to question whether information provided to her during interactions with patients, particularly that of a personal nature, could legitimately be used for research purposes. This could have been resolved by giving patients frequent reminders that the research was taking place. However, she felt that constantly highlighting the research would have adversely affected the unobtrusive nature of the research and ultimately the quality of the findings.

A related dilemma concerned the extent to which a patient's consent could be assumed to remain valid when their medical condition deteriorated such that they ceased to be the person they were when they gave initial consent. Lawton refers to a case of someone she calls 'Annie' who changed from being 'lively and talkative' when she first came into the hospice to being 'withdrawn and disengaged' as her condition deteriorated, so much so that she requested heavy sedation with the result that she was unable to communicate in the last two weeks of her life (Lawton, 2001: 700). Annie had given consent to the study on her admission to the hospice and was supportive of it. However, the fact that she was sedated meant that it was impossible to ascertain whether she wished to remain in the study once her condition deteriorated. Including people in the last stage of their life was important for the study because one of the study aims was to explore the impact of patients' deaths on other hospice patients. This case, and others like it, was important in informing the study findings which had organisational implications for the hospice. However, as Lawton (2001: 700) notes it is important to consider how Annie and others like her might have felt if they had known how their data were to be used.

The third set of dilemmas concern a different aspect of consent which relates to the ways in which, in qualitative research, the specific outcomes of research cannot be predicted. At the outset of a study, a general research focus and research question or set of research questions will generally have been designed but the number of study participants, the period of data collection and the specific direction the research will take is often dependent on the data collected and the emerging analysis. This has particular implications for consent. In common with other qualitative studies, Lawton's study evolved into something other than that for which participants originally gave their consent and her findings ended up critiquing the hospice movement. This left Lawton to pose the question whether patients would have consented to participate, and indeed whether hospice staff would have granted her access, had they known what the outcome of the research would be.

The dilemmas identified by Lawton centre around the need to conduct high-quality research that can provide answers to important research questions which will have the ability to impact on policy and practice but to do so in ways that respect research participants' wishes as well as their dignity. Lawton managed these dilemmas, not by continual checking of consent in relation to the data collected and used, but by careful and selective use of the data collected. She notes (Lawton, 2001: 699):

> Researchers who employ this methodology have a responsibility to use the data they collect in a sensitive, ethical and reflexive manner. In this project, every effort was made to quote patients and to use specific case studies in a highly selective fashion. The experiences of many patients were only drawn on in abstract ways, for example, in developing the generalized themes and trends that were highlighted in the study.

case study

Dilemmas of disclosure: Michael Rowe

Michael Rowe's research was a study of British policing (Rowe, 2007). Using ethnographic methods, he accompanied uniformed police officers as they went about their normal duties in three areas within one police service. The aims of this study were to explore the factors that shape officers' decision-making and their exercise of discretion. His research involved accompanying and observing police in their day-to-day activities over a period of 18 weeks and taking field notes of his observations. Rowe (2007) identifies a number of ethical issues that emerged from his research but the focus here is on two specific incidents which presented him with ethical dilemmas. These two incidents centre around issues of role conflict, namely if and when a researcher should report an incident they are concerned with which will result in breaking confidentiality and/or affecting the very thing a researcher has set out to observe. Rowe noted that his reading of ethnographic studies of policing led him to expect to find malpractice that would lead to serious ethical dilemmas. In fact the situations he observed were comparatively minor but nevertheless did cause concern. A full discussion of the issues outlined below can be found in Rowe (2007).

The most significant incident that Rowe observed concerned an incident in which a police officer lied to a victim of crime. The 'victim' was a woman with learning difficulties who reported the theft of a mobile phone by a young man known to her. The officer said that he would go and talk to the person she had accused of stealing her phone. However, the officer told the researcher that he thought that the mobile phone may not have been stolen at all and that the woman may have lent it to the person she accused of stealing it and he had simply not returned it as agreed. Even if this were not the case he thought that the young man would probably lie and say that it was. Either way it was felt that the woman would not be a 'credible witness' due to her learning disability and, given the incident was minor, it was not likely to lead to any criminal proceedings. The officer decided that he would tell the woman that he had spoken to the young man's mother and that she would get him to return the phone to her once he arrived home even though this was not the case. The officer noted:

There's no point making a crime report, or a statement. We would
get the same result after two hours' paperwork, so why bother?
(Rowe, 2007: 46)

Rowe was very surprised by this incident, both the fact that the
officer had lied and also that he had been open to the researcher about
it. The incident was viewed as particularly troubling because the victim
of the crime had learning difficulties. He decided that three options
were available to him: to do nothing; to discuss the matter with the
officer; or, to report it to a more senior officer. The first of these would
protect his position as a researcher because he was not intervening
but would mean he was colluding with the officer's behaviour which
fell short of official stated police standards. The second might impact
negatively on the relationship developed by the researcher with the
officers he was studying and might result in officers limiting the
activities that he was able to observe or censoring their behaviour
while he was observing. The third option would be likely to result
in significant consequences in relation to the ongoing research and
relationships with officers as well as the additional problem that he
would be breaching confidentiality and also run the risk of spoiling
the field for other researchers. Rowe decided not to report the incident
primarily because he felt the seriousness of the officer's behaviour
did not outweigh the likely consequences of reporting it. He notes
that if an officer had committed an offence of a more serious nature a
different decision might have to be taken.

A second incident, which did not involve criticism of an officer,
was managed in rather a different way. In this incident, the researcher
observed a suspect put something in his mouth and swallow it.
This occurred outside of the view of an officer. The researcher was
concerned that the suspect may have swallowed drugs, an action that
might have a detrimental impact on them and the officer. At the same
time, however, from a methodological point of view, he did not want to
interfere with the situation and influence events but rather to observe
what would naturally unfold if he was not present. However, he
decided that the potential impact on the suspect and the officer were
primary and so he told the officer what he had seen.

The dilemmas identified by Rowe centre around a similar issue to
that identified by Lawton, that of how to manage ethical issues that
emerge in the context of naturalistic enquiry that seeks to minimise

the researcher's impact on the field. For Rowe, moral questions about whether to intervene and the consequences of such interventions for the research and those involved with it are dilemmas which have to be considered situationally, according to the severity of the incident. He notes (Rowe, 2007: 47, 48):

> This response was based on a calculation of outcome rather than the content of the action – and so reflects broader debates about the status of ethics in a postmodern era ... Since policing is unpredictable, the ethical dilemmas police researchers might face cannot be easily anticipated. Given this Norris's conclusion that ethics are inevitably situational (Norris, 1993) was borne out in this study. If an absolute code of ethics is not feasible, researchers must be prepared to be reflexive in terms of ethical dilemmas.

case study

case study

Dilemmas of confidentiality: Timescapes

A research project on young people's lives conducted by Edwards and Weller raised significant, and perhaps unusual, ethical dilemmas relating to confidentiality. The project was conducted as part of Timescapes, a UK programme of qualitative longitudinal research projects. The focus of the project was on the meanings, experiences and changes over time in young people's relationships with siblings and friends. The study involved repeated interviews with young people born between 1989 and 1996. During the course of the final set of interviews, conducted during 2009, an ethical issue relating to confidentiality emerged following the unexpected death of one of the study participants. This raised some issues and dilemmas about consent but more importantly about confidentiality. The project researchers invited researchers involved in other Timescapes projects to contribute their thoughts about how these ethical dilemmas might be resolved. Details about these deliberations and the project more generally can be found here: http://www.timescapes.leeds.ac.uk/research-projects/siblings-friends

The sudden death of the research participant, Dan, raised ethical and legal issues concerning the data collected. While he had verbally agreed to all the data collected being archived, it had been intended to provide participants with more detailed information about archiving and asking them to sign 'consent to archiving' forms in the round of interviews that were due to take place at the time of his death. Edwards and Weller raised the question as to whether they could archive the data from Dan that they had already collected on the basis of his verbal consent given two years previously. They considered asking his parents to give consent but this raised further issues, such as whether this would mean that his parents had ownership over the data and what to do if they demanded their own copies of Dan's data, thereby overriding the promises of confidentiality given to Dan. Another issue was what to do if they refused permission despite Dan's verbal consent at an earlier stage which could be seen as overriding Dan's wishes. The researchers also identified a further moral issue relating to confidentiality. They felt that, given Dan's sudden and unexpected death, his parents would like to have, and perhaps should be provided with, some of the non-sensitive audio material they had collected from Dan during interviews. While making such an offer would go against promises of confidentiality made at the time of the interviews, this might be seen as acceptable given the circumstances, as long as the data provided were of a non-sensitive nature.

Edwards and Weller received eleven responses from fellow researchers within the Timescapes programme to the issues they raised, representing a range of views. Some researchers felt that there was no justification for overriding the promise of confidentiality given to Dan, while others felt the situation warranted the disclosure of non-sensitive data. The range of responses illustrates the lack of consensus about these issues among the social science community. Edwards and Weller note that there was no single solution to these ethical dilemmas. Drawing on an ethics of care perspective, they took what they felt to be the morally caring course of action. They decided that Dan's former verbal consent was adequate to enable them to archive Dan's data without consent from his parents. However, they offered his parents the opportunity to archive any personal memories they had of Dan alongside this. They also offered Dan's parents a sample of Dan's voice. Dan's parents wanted to take up this offer and were provided with a DVD of extracts from Dan's interview where he discussed his likes and his career aims.

The dilemmas identified by Edwards and Weller centre around the contexts in which agreements made, such as for consent, confidentiality and anonymity, might be breached. Their experience was relatively unusual, but not unheard of or without parallel. In their case, their views about what was the 'morally caring' course of action for all concerned which would, as far as they could be aware, not go against the wishes of their study participant defined the action they took.

Making ethical decisions

These case studies drawn from published research provide interesting and unusually detailed descriptions of ethical dilemmas raised by research in different contexts. They demonstrate that, in making ethical decisions, researchers frequently have to balance the quality of their research with the ethical treatment of their research participants and that at times there can be a conflict between these two aims. They illustrate how there is often not one clear solution to the ethical dilemmas that emerge in research but rather that decisions are situational and contextual. They also illustrate how other researchers, drawing on different moral frameworks, might resolve ethical dilemmas in different ways to the researchers in these case studies. In short, they illustrate that specific ethical issues may be viewed and justified differently according to the specific issue, the context and the researcher. Importantly, however, they illustrate the careful consideration and reflexivity that these researchers have employed in resolving their ethical dilemmas.

Summary

There are a number of ethical 'horror stories' in the social sciences. However, for the most part, researchers manage the ethical issues that emerge in considered and reflexive ways that enable them to conduct research which will produce valid findings while at the same time treating research participants with respect. The need for careful consideration, evaluation and justification of ethical decisions is central to good ethical decision-making.

7 Where next for research ethics?

Introduction

There have been several developments in research methods over the last decade or so which have, arguably, significantly changed the nature of the way in which many social scientists conduct research and consequently the ethical issues with which they engage. In this chapter, trends and developments in qualitative research methods and the ethical issues that they raise are outlined. The chapter concludes by discussing whether these ethical issues demand new approaches to research ethics or involve the re-working of familiar issues in new contexts. It also outlines some ideas about the direction for research ethics in the future.

Developments in research methods

The last decade or so has seen a rapid growth in the development and use of a number of specific methodological approaches in qualitative research. These include: narrative, biographical and performative methods; visual and creative methods; participatory methods; digital and e-research, and data sharing. Some of these developments reflect what has been termed the 'cultural turn' in the social sciences and the interest in identity, while others reflect what has been referred to as the democratisation of research and the moves to the involvement and empowerment of research participants. The rapid growth in digital technology, changes in the ways that people interact online and the scope that online communications provide for understanding aspects of the social world are another factor involved in some of these developments. A further factor is the need to ensure data sharing in the interests of maximising value from research and providing datasets and resources of value to future researchers. It has been observed that the developments outlined here have been driven by a number of factors, such as advances in technology and cross-fertilisation across disciplines (Xenitidou and Gilbert, 2009). Some of the developments in each of these methods and approaches and the major corresponding ethical issues they raise are explored below. In this brief outline to each of these methodological areas it is possible to identify only very general issues. It is of course the case that the ethical issues that arise within each of these methodological approaches are contextual and will vary according to the nature of the project.

Narrative methods

The use of narrative methods has increased markedly over the last two decades (see Elliott, 2005; Squire, 2008). Narrative methods encompass a wide range of approaches, including event-based narratives, narratives of experience and perfomative and cultural narratives; the first two of these focus on the content of people's narrative and the latter on the structure and form of narratives. Other forms of narrative approaches include biographical research, life history research and oral history (see Plummer, 2001). The methods employed in qualitative narrative research include the collection of data via interview and observation, generally over prolonged periods, as well as analysis of a range of documentary sources. Key elements of narrative approaches are that they involve researchers enabling research participants to tell stories about their lives, that researchers need to pay close attention to and value respondents' stories, that researchers develop close relationships with their study participants and that they form part of the narratives that are constructed. All these elements highlight the need for reflexivity in narrative research.

Numerous ethical issues have been identified as arising from narrative, life history and biographical approaches. Plummer (2001: 216) identifies seven ethical 'concerns' in life history approaches (see also Elliott, 2005; Squire, 2008). Primary among these are issues of exploitation, risk of harm, anonymity and confidentiality and ownership. Plummer (2001) identifies exploitation as perhaps the most crucial issue in that study participants are encouraged to provide their personal, and perhaps painful, stories but that it is the researcher that benefits, both professionally and materially, from the reporting of these stories in which the subject of the narrative is anonymised and generally receives no credit or reimbursement. The risk of harm is also significant in narrative research. As Elliott (2005: 137) notes, people's narratives are bound up with their sense of identity and the process of data collection and the interpretation and dissemination of these narratives can, if done insensitively, cause considerable harm to individuals and their relatives, friends and communities. Plummer develops this theme by arguing that (2001: 224):

> Telling their stories could literally destroy them – bring them to suicidal edges, murderous thoughts, danger. More modestly, they may be severely traumatised. The telling of a story of life is a deeply problematic and ethical process in which researchers are fully implicated.

Issues of confidentiality and anonymity are also particularly problematic in narrative and biographical research in that these methods often render participants identifiable, or at least potentially so. Often participants are identified in the publication of material, with their consent, but this is not without the sorts of problems discussed in chapter 3. This then raises issues about what can, or should, be confidential in such studies and how such material should be managed.

Narrative approaches appear to raise some specific ethical challenges in relation to the management of relationships with study participants and sensitive handling of their stories. The specific issues raised reflect those in qualitative research more broadly and mirror the traditional areas of concern of research ethics: those of confidentiality, anonymity and risk of harm. Plummer (2001: 228) argues for dealing with them through a postmodern ethics that is grounded in researchers' day-to-day practices but one that is not divorced from broader ethical and moral principles.

Visual and creative methods

There has been a rapid growth in interest in visual research methods over the last decade or so across a range of social science disciplines and research settings. 'Visual methods' comprise a vast array of different types of approaches and data. Visual data include photographs, film, video, drawings, advertisements or media images, sketches, graphical representations and models created by a range of creative media. Prosser and Loxley (2008) identify four different types of visual data: 'found data' (for example family photograph albums); 'researcher created data' (such as images or film taken by researchers); 'respondent created data' (such as models or drawings created by respondents) and 'representations' (for example graphical representations of data).

Visual methods raise a number of ethical issues. Perhaps the primary issue centres around the use of material in which individuals are recognisable, or potentially recognisable, and the challenges this raises in relation to issues of anonymity, confidentiality and consent (see chapter 4). Consent should be obtained for taking and using such images. However, this in itself is not always straightforward in that it may not be possible to obtain consent for all people in images and, even if consent is obtained, respondents may not be able to fully appreciate what the implications of being identified may be. The fact that it is increasingly the preference of both researchers and respondents that study participants are *not* anonymised in visual research findings raises a further set of ethical considerations, not least that this presents a challenge to established ethical practice. Wider ethical issues have also been identified concerning the way that images are constructed by researchers and consumed by those who view them (Rose, 2007: 255). This has drawn attention to the ethical implications, and consequences for individuals and their communities, of the ways in which researchers present images and the interpretations different audiences may make. Many established 'visual' researchers tend to adopt participatory or collaborative relationships with their study participants so that the materials created emerge from collaborations between them and are seen as jointly owned (Banks, 2001; Gold, 1989; Pink, 2007). Nevertheless the potential remains for participants in studies that use visual material (as with all research) to be unhappy about the way they have been portrayed (Pink, 2003; Crow and Wiles, 2008).

Prosser has argued that visual research methods sit uneasily within conventional ethical practice and regulation in social research and that this poses problems in relation to the review of visual research by research ethics committees or boards (Prosser, 2000; Wiles *et al*, 2011). Proponents of visual research have noted the importance of visual researchers developing ethical practice and becoming members of the committees or boards which conduct ethical review to improve the ethical review and decision-making processes in relation to visual research (Pauwels, 2008). The ethical issues raised by visual research are similar to those raised by all research, primarily those of consent, confidentiality and anonymity.

Participatory methods

Interest in participatory research approaches has grown significantly in the last twenty years. This has been fuelled, in part, by pressure from particular groups of 'service users' for involvement in the research that informs their treatment, care and experiences as well as from researchers working in specific fields such as gender studies, childhood studies, ethnic studies and disability studies who have identified the importance of empowering participants. The resulting insistence by some grant-giving bodies for 'user involvement' in research has meant that most researchers working in health and social care in Britain have to have at least some element of involvement from members of the population they are researching in the design and/or conduct of their research. Participatory approaches are most commonly used in research with children and young people (see, for example, Renold *et al*, 2008), research with a range of 'service users', including people with physical and learning disabilities (see, for example, Tarleton *et al*, 2004), and research on community and/or community development (see, for example, Lassiter *et al.*, 2004). There are various participatory research methodologies including participatory action research, participatory rural appraisal, participatory mapping and participatory video but in the main participatory research is distinguished by the level of collaboration between researcher and participants. The levels of involvement that research participants might have with a research project range from consultation, through to collaboration and full control by research participants (Involve 2004; Frankham, 2009). Participatory research is characterised by the involvement of research participants across all stages of a research project.

Researchers using participatory approaches foreground ethical issues as part of their approach. The key ethical issues identified focus primarily around the power differentials between participants and researchers. Frankham (2009) identifies the key ethical issues for researchers attempting to involve service users in research as being tensions around the ownership and authorship of research and the related issues of accountability and remuneration. Similar issues are reflected on by Tarleton *et al* (2004) in relation to research with people with learning disabilities and by Heath *et al* (2009: 73) in relation to research with children and young people. Informed consent has also been identified as a particular challenge in relation to research with children and young people because of the often longitudinal nature of participatory research and the fluid nature of the interactions between researcher and participant. Renold *et al* (2008), for example, found that in their longitudinal project on children and young people in the care of the local authority they had to devise various strategies to render participation visible throughout the project.

One of the challenges of participatory approaches is that researchers' interactions with their participants are not fixed. This is true for all qualitative research but more markedly so in relation to participatory approaches, when the direction of a study, the specific methods used and the dissemination strategy is always in a state of negotiation. This can create tensions in relation to processes of ethical review which operates on the basis of anticipated ethical issues. As Renold *et al* (2008: 443) note in relation to their research on 'looked-after children', participatory research ethics is not so much about 'multiple negotiated dilemmas'; rather it involves an 'ongoing dialogue in the micro-complexities inherent in everyday fieldwork relations'.

Digital and e-research

Possibly the most significant developments in research methods in the last decade relate to various forms of digital, online and e-research. The majority of the population in the Western World use the internet and increasingly a significant part of social interaction occurs online, particularly for some social groups (Dutton and Blank, 2011). The scope for making use of the internet in research has been widely recognised; Eynon *et al* (2008) note that the internet can be seen as a huge 'social science laboratory'. The ability to collect and combine various types of online and offline digital qualitative and quantitative data is a further development which has generated considerable research activity. Many of the developments in research using digital and online data are quantitative or draw on mixed methods approaches. The development of software tools to analyse activity on the internet, across sites or on specific sites has resulted in a growth in 'webometric' research (see for example Thelwall and Sud, 2012). Research has also been conducted in virtual environments such as 'Second Life' where behavioural experiments have been conducted through the use of avatars (Eynon *et al*, 2009). This type of research has significant ethical implications but, as the methods employed are largely quantitative, they will not be specifically discussed here. Rather the focus is on the challenges arising from relatively recent developments arising from what has been referred to as 'Web 2.0', primarily focusing on data from social networking sites and other user generated content such as blogs (Snee, 2008). Research on social networking and blogging has used ethnographic methods within sites, often in combination with quantitative methods such as social network analysis (see Eynon *et al*, 2009; Snee, 2008).

The primary ethical issue arising from these developments and online research in general relate to the issues of privacy and consent (see also chapter 3). It was noted in chapter 3 that distinguishing between what is public and private on the web is problematic. Snee (2008) notes the nature of the Web 2.0 environment complicates this further in that social networking sites encourage the sharing of personal and even intimate information. The extent to which such information is viewed by the author as being in the public domain is not necessarily easy to gauge. There are also issues relating to anonymity because, even if people or institutions are anonymised in research reports, information collected from the internet is often easily traceable via a search engine. Identifying when anonymity should be used and when it is appropriate to cite an internet user as an author by name is again not straightforward. It is certainly the case that not all internet users want to remain anonymous; this may apply particularly to authors of blogs, and to anonymise people in such circumstances could be seen as infringing copyright and raise issues of intellectual property. Issues of consent are also potentially problematic, as has been discussed in chapter 3. All these issues are complicated by the fact that in online research geographical boundaries do not exist and thus different legal and ethical regulation applies to the data collected.

In common with the concerns raised by researchers using visual methods, it has been noted that ethical review committees lack knowledge about Web 2.0 and that researchers may need to educate committee members as well as the wider research community. Eynon *et al* (2008: 26) note that despite concerns that online research raises specific ethical challenges, there has more recently been a convergence in the view that research ethics for online research can be drawn from existing frameworks for offline settings. Similarly Snee (2008: 20) found that most internet researchers did not feel that a specific 'Web 2.0' ethics is needed. Nevertheless it is recognised that some special considerations are necessary when researching online and that issues of confidentiality, anonymity, disclosure, informed consent and privacy are cast in a different light in online research.

Data sharing

In the last decade or so there has been a marked increase in the development of policies to promote or recommend data sharing; this is increasingly a requirement on the part of research funders (Van den Eynden *et al*, 2009). In the UK the qualitative data archive, Qualidata, was established in 1994 (becoming part of the UK Data Archive in 2001) and similar developments have occurred in the US and Europe to enable the sharing and re-use of data from qualitative research (see Corti and Thompson, 2007). In part this development reflects a financial imperative for data sharing in order to achieve better value for money for research funders and avoid duplication of research effort. However, data sharing also provides researchers with opportunities to gain methodological and substantive insights from existing research data. Corti and Thompson (2007) identify six approaches to reusing data: description; comparative research, re-study or follow-up study; re-analysis or secondary analysis; research design or methodological advancement; verification; and, teaching and learning.

It has been noted that archiving for the purposes of data sharing raises significant ethical challenges. Neale and Bishop (2012a) argue that these occur because the priorities and interests of the various parties involved do not necessarily coincide. Balancing the rights and responsibilities of the primary researcher and the research team, secondary researchers who want to make use of the data, the data archivist, research participants, research funders and the general public may present significant challenges. The central issues revolve around informed consent, confidentiality and anonymity.

To ensure that research participants give consent for data archiving and re-use, it is essential that this explicitly forms part of the consent process. Gaining informed consent for data sharing and re-use is particularly problematic in that researchers and their participants do not know what future uses will be made of these data; it is impossible to know what questions researchers will ask of the dataset and how long in the future such secondary analysis may take place. It is possible that secondary research may be conducted in ways that the primary researcher and the research participants are unhappy about. While these concerns may be responded to by restricting access arrangements for data so that researchers have to register for access to the data and to comply with specific arrangements for viewing the data (such as having to register for its use and to use it only in non-public environments), it is far harder to justify limiting the ways in which secondary researchers analyse these data. Arguably it is not in the interests of the research community, research funders and the general public to limit the uses that can be made of research, especially where it is publicly funded. Neale and Bishop (2012b) argue that researchers have a duty to protect their research participants but they have to balance this with a wider responsibility to the research community and the public and that they need to work closely with their participants to make this explicit in the case of data sharing.

Researchers themselves are also vulnerable to criticism from other researchers as a result of archiving their research data. Neale and Bishop (2012b) note that researchers undertaking secondary analysis may criticise a primary researcher's ways of working or not take account of the different cultural and intellectual environments in which these data were produced. They argue that both secondary and primary researchers have ethical responsibilities to adopt an ethics of care approach in their dealings with each other so that the primary researcher acknowledges the rights of the secondary researcher to analyse their data as they see fit but that this should occur in ways that respect the integrity of the primary researcher's original work.

Issues of anonymity and confidentiality are also prominent in relation to archiving and data sharing. Ensuring confidentiality through processes of anonymisation is important but at the same time the integrity of the data needs to be protected to ensure its utility. The usefulness of data can be undermined if relational information, geographical references or alterations to aural or visual data are made such that its value to secondary researchers is minimal. Neale and Bishop (2012b) note that while researchers have a duty to protect participants they also have a responsibility to get their accounts heard as widely as possible. Managing this issue involves balancing these competing responsibilities.

Where next for research ethics?

Researchers working in each of the methodological approaches outlined above have identified the specific ethical challenges raised. The topics relate, broadly, to the general issues identified in traditional qualitative approaches and discussed in the various ethical and moral research ethics frameworks presented in chapter 2; those of anonymity and confidentiality, informed consent, and risk of harm. This is perhaps not surprising given that this is the framework by which ethical questions in social research are addressed. Nevertheless, some of the specific issues identified within these broad ethical topics imply, to a greater or lesser extent, a re-framing of traditional approaches to ethics. This is perhaps particularly pertinent in relation to the issue of anonymity. In all five approaches discussed above some challenges to the need for anonymity are raised. This is a view supported by many researchers, particularly visual and participatory researchers, who argue that research participants often want to be identified and should have the right to be, providing this does not pose risks to their or other participants' well-being (Grinyer, 2002; Wiles *et al*, 2011). Tilley and Woodthorpe (2011) argue that the concept of anonymity may be inappropriate in the context of twenty-first century qualitative research activity. They note that anonymity can conflict with demands to disseminate widely, particularly on the internet which poses various threats to anonymity. They also note that anonymity can conflict with the wishes of funding bodies and with knowledge transfer to policy-makers and practitioners. It seems likely that it is in the area of anonymity that the greatest challenge to traditional research ethics will occur in the future.

A further important issue raised by the review of the above approaches is that research ethics committees and regulation more broadly are viewed by many people as curtailing or limiting research using these approaches. It is argued that members of ethics committees lack understanding of non-traditional methods and that researchers using, for example, visual and online approaches, need to educate them to ensure that this does not pose a challenge to such research being conducted. These criticisms form part of a wider critique of the ethical governance and regulation of the social sciences in the UK and elsewhere (Atkinson, 2009; Hammersley, 2009). Criticisms of the regulation of research in the UK have thus far had limited impact on what has been referred to as 'ethics creep'. It seems probable that debates about the merits of regulation, and perhaps also resistance to it, will remain a feature of social science research into the foreseeable future (see Stanley and Wise, 2010).

One of the key issues that researchers using the approaches outlined above identify is the need for situational relativist approaches to be adopted in managing the ethical issues that emerge in research rather than adherence to a set of principles or rules. Adherence to principle and rule-based ethical frameworks appears to be identified as particularly challenging in relation to these developing and emerging research approaches. This is a key debate in the research ethics literature and one which, arguably, lies at the heart of concerns about regulation. Plummer (2001: 226) regards the distinction between ethical absolutists (who view ethical principles as important in driving ethical decision-making) and situational relativists (who view ethical decision-making as emerging from an individual researcher's moral framework) as an unhelpful dichotomy. His argument, consistent with the one which I have put forward in this book (see chapter 2), is that ethical decision-making needs to be guided by an ethical framework. Such frameworks do not *determine* decision-making but rather provide researchers with a means of thinking systematically about moral behaviour in research.

Summary

The last decade or so has seen a rapid growth in the development and use of a number of specific methodological approaches in qualitative research. These include: narrative, biographical and performative methods; visual and creative methods; participatory methods; digital and e-research, and data sharing. Some of the ethical issues raised by these approaches imply a re-framing of traditional approaches to ethics. This is perhaps particularly pertinent in relation to the issue of anonymity. Research ethics committees and regulation more broadly are viewed as curtailing or limiting research using these approaches. It seems likely that debates about the merits and form of regulation will remain a feature of social science research in the foreseeable future.

Further reading and resources

General guidance on research ethics

There are a number of useful books and websites which provide an introduction to research ethics, discussion of the key issues that need consideration and guidance on the process of gaining ethical approval for a research project.

The online resource called the Research Ethics Guidebook is particularly aimed at helping researchers navigate a range of regulatory procedures but also provides up-to-date information on ethical issues that occur across all stages of the research process. http://www.ethicsguidebook. ac.uk/

The BBC Ethics webpage provides an accessible introduction to ethics in general (not research ethics specifically) which outlines the various ethical approaches. http://www.bbc.co.uk/ethics/introduction/

The Social Science Research Ethics Website developed by Lancaster University provides a range of helpful resources exploring key ethical themes including ethical issues relating to research in global contexts, research with vulnerable groups and participatory research. http:// www.lancs.ac.uk/researchethics/

An online resource developed by the Realities research group at the University of Manchester highlights some of the ethical issues that emerge when working in teams and suggests some helpful approaches to ethical working relationships. Realities Toolkit 6 *After the Ethical Approval Form: Ethical considerations of working in research teams* http://www.socialsciences.manchester.ac.uk/morgancentre/realities/toolkits/research-team-ethics/index.html

Two introductory books to research ethics which are particularly useful are:

Iphofen, R. (2009), *Ethical Decision Making in Social Research*, Basingstoke: Palgrave Macmillan. This book provides a practical guide to ethical decision-making, including processes of obtaining ethical approval.
Gregory, I. (2003), *Ethics in Research*, London: Continuum. This book provides a short and useful introduction to research ethics.

The following books explore a range of ethical issues in some depth:

Israel, M. & Hay, I. (2006), *Research Ethics for Social Scientists*, London: Sage.
Mertens, D. & Ginsberg, P. (eds.) (2009), *The Handbook of Social Research Ethics*, California: Sage.
Van den Hoonard, W. (ed.) (2002), *Walking the Tightrope: Ethical Issues for Qualitative Researchers*, Toronto: University of Toronto Press.

Most of the above books and resources discuss the various moral and ethical frameworks for thinking about research ethics. The following books explore some of the specific ethical positions or frameworks:

Beauchamp, T. & Childress, J. (2001), *Principles of Biomedical Ethics*, New York: Oxford University Press. This book is the key handbook for principlist approaches. While it was developed primarily for medical ethics, it is widely used as the basis for social science ethics.
Macfarlane, B. (2009), *Researching with Integrity*, New York: Routledge. This book provides a detailed exploration of virtue ethics and identifies the moral virtues, and corresponding vices, that the virtuous researcher should ideally adopt at different stages of the research process.
Mauthner, M., Birch, M., Jessop, J. & Miller, T. (eds.) (2002), *Ethics in Qualitative Research*, London: Sage. This book explores ethical issues from a feminist ethics of care approach.

Risks and safety

Useful publications relating to risk and safety of research participants and researchers are:

Bloor, M., Fincham, B. and Sampson, H. (2007), *Qualiti (NCRM) Commissioned Inquiry into the Risk to Well-Being of Researchers in Qualitative Research.* http://www.cardiff.ac.uk/socsi/qualiti/ publications.html This report provides a comprehensive exploration of risks in relation to researchers and of how such risks can and should be managed.

SRA (2003), *A Code of Practice for the Safety of Social Researchers.* Available from: http://www.the-sra.org.uk/guidelines.htm This provides some useful guidance for enhancing researcher safety.

Lee, R. (1993), *Doing Research on Sensitive Topics*, London: Sage. This book reviews studies on sensitive topics and explores (among other ethical issues) some of the risks of undertaking such research for both researchers and their participants.

Consent

General books on ethics all discuss issues of consent; the following books and resources focus specifically on this issue.

Smyth, M. & Williamson, E. (eds.) (2004), *Researchers and Their 'Subjects': Ethics, Power, Knowledge and Consent*, Bristol: Policy Press.

Wiles, R., Health, S., Crow, G. and Charles, V. (2008), *Informed Consent in Social Research: A Literature Review.* http://eprints.ncrm.ac.uk/85/

Informed Consent and the Research Process project web page http:// www.sociology.soton.ac.uk/Proj/Informed_Consent/index.htm

Ethical issues in relation to specific methods

There are a number of resources that focus on ethical issues in online or e-research. Particularly useful are the following:

http://www.restore.ac.uk/orm/site/home.htm This website has an extensive section on online research ethics which includes resources, reading lists and training materials.

http://www.oii.ox.ac.uk/publications/ The Oxford Internet Institute also has a number of publications on ethical issues in online and e-research.

There are also resources relating to ethical issues in visual methods, for example:

Wiles, R., Prosser, J., Bagnoli, A., Clark, A., Davies, K., Holland, S. and Renold, E. (2008), *Visual Ethics: Ethical Issues in Visual Research.* http://eprints.ncrm.ac.uk/421/

There are also numerous resources relating to the archiving of qualitative data and the ethical issues in archiving and the re-use of data available from the UK Qualidata archive at: http://www.esds.ac.uk/qualidata/
The UK Timescapes projects has also produced various guidelines relating to the ethics of archiving and reusing qualitative longitudinal data, for example: Neale, B. and Bishop, L. 'The ethics of archiving and re-using qualitative longitudinal data: a stakeholder approach.' *Timescapes Methods Guides Series. Guide no 18.* Available at: http://www.timescapes.leeds.ac.uk

Professional guidelines and codes

All the social science discipline-specific organisations have guidelines or codes of ethical conduct which can be accessed from their websites. In addition, the Social Research Association has produced ethical guidelines for social researchers that are relevant across sectors of work and disciplines. These are accessible via their website (www.the-sra.org.uk). The EU RESPECT guidelines (http://www.respectproject.org/code/) are relevant for social and economic researchers working in EU countries. These are a synthesis of professional and ethical codes of practice and legal requirements across the EU.

The Economic and Social Research Council (ESRC) Framework for Research Ethics (http://www.esrc.ac.uk/about-esrc/information/research-ethics.aspx) provides a code of conduct for social research. Compliance with this is mandatory for research funded by the ESRC and recommended for research funded by other bodies.

References

Adler, P. A. and Adler, P. (2002), 'The reluctant respondent', in Gubrium, J. and Holstein, J. (eds.) *Handbook of Interview Research: Context and Method*, California: Sage.

Alderson, P. (2004), 'Ethics', in Fraser, S., Lewis, V., Ding, S., Kellett, M. and Robinson, C. (eds.), *Doing Research with Children and Young People*, London: Sage.

Allmark, P. (2002), 'The ethics of research with children', *Nurse Researcher*, December 2002.

American Sociological Association (1999), *Code of Ethics and Policies and Procedures of the ASA Committee of Professional Ethics*, Washington DC, US: American Sociological Association. http://www2.asanet.org/members/ecoderev.html

Association of Social Anthropologists of the UK and the Commonwealth (2011), Ethical Guidelines for good research practice. Available from: http://www.theasa.org/ethics.shtml

Atkinson, P. (2009), Ethics and ethnography, *21st Century Society: Journal of the Academy of Social Sciences*, *4* (1): 17–30.

Back, L. (2004), 'Listening with our eyes: portraiture as urban encounter', in Knowles, C. & Sweetman, P. (eds.) *Picturing the Social Landscape: Visual Methods and the Sociological Imagination* (pp.132–146), London: Routledge.

Banks, M. (2001), *Visual Methods in Social Research*, London: Sage.

BBC Ethics webpage http://www.bbc.co.uk/ethics/introduction/

Beauchamp, T. and Childress, J. (1979), *Principles of Biomedical Ethics*, New York: Oxford University Press.

Beauchamp, T. and Childress, J. (2001), *Principles of Biomedical Ethics*, New York: Oxford University Press.

Becker, S. and Bryman, A. (2004), *Understanding Research for Social Policy and Practice: Themes, Methods and approaches*, Bristol: Policy Press.

Bengry-Howell, A. and Griffin, C. (2011), 'Negotiating access in ethnographic research with "hard to reach" young people: establishing common ground or a process of methodological grooming?', *International Journal of Social Research Methodology* DOI: 10.1080/13645579.2011.600115

Bloor, M., Fincham, B. and Sampson, H. (2007), *Qualiti (NCRM) Commissioned Inquiry into the Risk to Well-Being of Researchers in Qualitative Research.* http://www.cardiff.ac.uk/socsi/qualiti/publications.html

Bostock, L. (2002), '"God, she's gonna report me": the ethics of child protection in poverty research', *Children and Society* 16: 273–283.

Boulton, M., Brown, N., Lewis, G. and Webster, A. (2004), 'Implementing the ESRC Research Ethics Framework: The Case for Research Ethics Committees', *ESRC Research Ethics Framework: Discussion Paper 4 (working paper)* http://www.york.ac.uk/res/ref/docs/REFpaper4_v2.pdf

Brannen, J. (1988), 'The study of sensitive subjects', *Sociological Review* 36: 352–63.

British Educational Research Association (2004), Revised Ethical Guidelines for Educational Research. http://www.bera.ac.uk/publications/ethical-guidelines

British Psychological Society (2007), Report of the Working Party on Conducting Research on the Internet: Guidelines for Ethical Practice in Psychological Research Online.

British Psychological Society (2009), *Code of Ethics and Conduct: Guidance published by the Ethics Committee of the British Psychological Society.* Leicester: British Psychological Society.

British Sociological Association, (2002) Statement of Ethical Practice for the British Sociological Association. http://www.britsoc.co.uk/about/equality/statement-of-ethical-practice.aspx

British Sociological Association – Visual Sociology Group's statement of ethical practice (2006). www.visualsociology.org.uk/about/ethical_statement.php

Cameron, A., Lloyd, L., Kent, N. and Anderson, P. (2004), 'Researching end of life in old age: ethical challenges', in Smyth, M. & Williamson, E. (eds) *Researchers and Their Subjects: Ethics, Power, Knowledge and Consent* Bristol: Policy Press.

Clark, A. (2006), Anonymising Research Data. ESRC National Centre for Research Methods Real Life Methods Node, University of Manchester Working Paper. http://www.reallifemethods.ac.uk/publications/workingpapers/

Clark, A., Prosser, J. and Wiles, R. (2010), 'Ethical issues in image-based research', *Arts and Health* 2, 1: 81–93.

Clarke, G., Boorman, G. and Nind, M. (2011), '"If they don't listen I shout, and when I shout they listen": hearing the voices of girls with behavioural, emotional and social difficulties', *British Educational Research Journal*, 37,5: 765–80.

Coomber, R. (2002), 'Signing your life away?: why Research Ethics Committees (REC) shouldn't always require written confirmation that participants in research have been informed of the aims of a study and their rights – the case of criminal populations (Commentary)', *Sociological Research Online* 7,1. http://www.socresonline.org.uk/7/1/coomber.html

Corden, A. and Sainsbury, R. (2006), *Using Verbatim Quotations in Reporting Qualitative Social Research: The views of research users*, Social Policy Research Unit, University of York, York.

Corden, A., Sainsbury, R., Sloper, P. and Ward, B. (2005), 'Using a model of group psychotherapy to support social research on sensitive topics', *International Journal of Social Research Methodology* 8, 2: 151–160.

Corti, L. and Thompson, P. (2007), 'Secondary analysis of archived data', in Seale, C., Gobo, G., Gubrium, J. and Sliverman, D. *Qualitative Research Practice*, London: Sage.

Crow, G. and Wiles, R. (2008), 'Managing anonymity and confidentiality in social research: the case of visual data in Community research', NCRM Working Paper. ESRC National Centre for Research Methods. http://eprints.ncrm.ac.uk/459

Cutliffe, J. and Ramcharan, P. (2002), 'Levelling the playing field? Exploring the merits of the ethics-as-process approach for judging qualitative research proposals', *Qualitative Health Research* 12,7: 1000–1010.

Dingwall, R. (2008), 'The ethical case against ethical regulation in humanities and social science research', *21st Century Society: Journal of the Academy of Social Sciences*, 3 (1): 1–12.

Dutton, W.H., and Blank, G. (2011), Next Generation Users: The Internet in Britain, Oxford Internet Survey 2011, Oxford Internet Institute: University of Oxford.

DVRG (2004), 'Domestic violence and research ethics, in Smyth, M. and Williamson, E. (eds) *Researchers and Their Subjects: Ethics, Power, Knowledge and Consent,* Bristol: Policy Press.

Edwards, S., Ashcroft, R. and Kirchin, S. (2004), Research ethics committees: differences and moral judgement, *Bioethics* 18: 408–427.

Edwards, R. and Mauthner, M. (2002), 'Ethics and feminist research: theory and practice', in Mauthner, M., Birch, M., Jessop, J. and Miller, T. (eds.) *Ethics in Qualitative Research,* London: Sage.

Edwards, R. and Weller, S. (2009), Timescapes project one: ethical dilemma correspondence. http://www.timescapes.leeds.ac.uk/assets/files/PROJECT-1-ethical-dilemma-correspondence-2.pdf

Ellis, J. (2011), 'Young people with autism: a case study of methodological innovation in researching socially excluded groups', unpublished report prepared for PhD, University of Southampton.

Elliott, J. (2005), *Using Narrative in Social Research: Qualitative and Quantitative Approaches,* London: Sage.

ESRC (2005) *Research Ethics Framework,* ESRC. http://www.esrcsocietytoday.ac.uk/ESRCInfoCentre/Images/ESRC_Re_Ethics_Frame_tcm6–11291.pdf

ESRC (2010) *Framework for Research Ethics,* ESRC. http://www.esrc.ac.uk/_images/Framework_for_Research_Ethics_tcm8–4586.pdf

Ess, C. and the AOIR Ethics Working Committee (2002), Ethical Decision-Making and Internet Research: Recommendations from the AoIR Ethics Working Committee. http://aoir.org/documents/ethics-guide/

Eynon, R., Fry, J. and Schroeder, R. (2008), 'The Ethics of Internet Research', in Fielding, N., Lee, R. and Blank, G. (eds.) The Sage Handbook of Online Research Methods, London: Sage.

Eynon, R., Schroeder, R. and Fry, J. (2009), 'New techniques in online research: challenges for research ethics', *Twenty First Century Society,* 4,2: 187–199.

European Science Foundation (2011), The European Code of Conduct for Research Integrity. http://www.esf.org/activities/mo-fora/research-integrity.html

Flewitt, R. (2005), 'Conducting research with young children: some ethical Considerations', *Early Child Development and Care,* 175, 6: 553–565.

Frankham, J. (2009), *Partnership research: a review of approaches and challenges in conducting research in partnership with service users*, ESRC National Centre for Research Methods Review paper. http://eprints. ncrm.ac.uk/778/

Gilligan, C. (1982), *In a Different Voice: Psychological Theory and Women's Development*, Cambridge, MA: Harvard University Press.

Gold, S. (1989), 'Ethical issues in visual fieldwork', in Blank, G., McCartney, J. and Brent, E. (eds.) *New Technology in Sociology: Practical Applications in Research and Work*, (pp. 99–109), New Brunswick, NJ, Transaction.

Goodenough, T., Williamson, E., Kent, J. and Ashcroft, R. (2004), 'Ethical protection in research: including children in the debate', in Smyth, M. and Williamson, E. (eds), *Researchers and Their Subjects: Ethics, Power, Knowledge and Consent*, Bristol: Policy Press.

Gregory, I. (2003), *Ethics in Research*, London: Continuum.

Griffin, C. and Bengry-Howell, A. (2008), 'Ethnography', in Willig, C. and Stainton-Rogers, W. *The Sage Handbook of Qualitative Research in Psychology*, London: Sage.

Grinyer, A. (2001), 'Ethical dilemmas in nonclinical health research from a UK perspective', *Nursing Ethics* 8, 2: 123–131.

Grinyer, A. (2002), 'The anonymity of research participants: assumptions, ethics and practicalities', *Social Research Update* Issue 36.

Haggerty, K. (2004), 'Ethics creep: governing social science research in the name of ethics', *Qualitative Sociology*, 27, 4: 391–414

Hammersley, M. (2009), 'Against the ethicists: on the evils of ethical regulation', *International Journal of Social Research Methodology*, 12, 3: 211–226.

Hammersley, M. (2010), 'Creeping ethical regulation and the strangling of research', *Sociological Research Online*, 15 (4) 16.

Haney, C., Banks, W. C., and Zimbardo, P. G. (1973), 'Interpersonal dynamics in a simulated prison', *International Journal of Criminology and Penology*, 1, 69–97.

Harper, D. (1998), 'An argument for visual sociology', in Prosser, J. (ed.) *Image-Based Research: A Sourcebook for Qualitative Researchers*, London: Routledge Falmer.

Heath, S., Brooks, R., Cleaver, E. and Ireland, E. (2009), *Researching Young People's Lives*, London: Sage

Held, V. (2006), *The Ethics of Care: Personal, Political, Global*, New York: Oxford University Press.

Herrera, C.D (1999), 'Two arguments for "covert methods" in social research', *British Journal of Sociology*, 5, 2, 331–343.

Hochschild, A. (1983), *The Managed Heart: The Commercialization of Human Feeling*, Berkeley: The University of California Press.

Holliday, R. (2004), 'Reflecting the self', in Knowles, C. and Sweetman, P. (2004), *Picturing the Social Landscape: Visual Methods and the Sociological Imagination*, London: Routledge.

Homan, R. (1991), *The Ethics of Social Research*, Longman: London.

Homan R. and Bulmer, M. (1982), 'On the merits of covert methods: a dialogue', in Bulmer, M. (ed.) *Social Research Ethics*, London: Macmillan Press.

Hope, T. (2004), *Medical Ethics: A Very Short Introduction*, Oxford: Oxford University Press.

Hooley, T., Marriott, J. and Wellens, J. (2012), *What is Online Research: Using the Internet for Social Science Research*, London: Bloomsbury.

Humphreys, L. (1975), *The Tea Room trade: Impersonal Sex in Public Places*, New York: Aldine de Gruyter.

INVOLVE (2004), *Involving the public in NHS, public health and social care research: briefing notes for researchers*, Eastleigh: INVOLVE.

Iphofen, R. (2009), *Ethical Decision Making in Social Research*, Basingstoke: Palgrave Macmillan.

Israel, M. (2004), *Ethics and the Governance of Criminological Research in Australia*, New South Wales Bureau of Crime Statistics and Research, Sydney.

Israel, M. and Hay, I. (2006), *Research Ethics for Social Scientists*, London: Sage.

Johnson, B. and Macleod Clark, J. (2003), 'Collecting sensitive data: the impact on researchers', *Qualitative Health Research*, 12(3): 421–434.

Kent, J., Williamson, E., Goodenough, T. and Ashcroft, R. (2002), 'Social science gets the ethics treatment: research governance and ethical review', *Sociological Research Online*, Vol 7, No. 4. http://socresonline.org.uk/7/4/williamson.html

Kenyon, E. and Hawker, S. (1999), '"Once would be enough": some reflections on the issue of safety for lone researchers', *International Journal of Social Research Methodology*, 2, 4: 313–327.

Kitchener, K. and Kitchener, R. (2009), 'Social science research ethics: historical and philosophical issues', in Mertens, D. and Ginsberg, P. (eds.) (2009), *The Handbook of Social Research Ethics*, California: Sage.

Kozinets, R. (2010), *Netnography: Doing Ethnographic Research Online*, London: Sage.

Langston, A., Abbott, L., Lewis, V. and Kellett, M. (2004), 'Early childhood', in Fraser, S., Lewis, V., Ding, S., Kellett, M. and Robinson, C. (eds.), *Doing Research with Children and Young People*, London: Sage.

Lassiter, L., Goodall, H., Campbell, E. and Johnson, M. (eds.) (2004), *The Other Side of Middletown: Exploring Muncie's African American Community*, Walnut Creek: Alta Mira Press.

Lawton, J. (2001), 'Gaining and maintaining consent: ethical concerns raised in a study of dying patients', *Qualitative Health Research*, 11,5: 693–705.

Lee, R. (1993), *Doing Research on Sensitive Topics*, London: Sage.

Lee, R. (1995), *Dangerous Fieldwork*, London: Sage.

Macfarlane, B. (2009), *Researching with Integrity*, New York: Routledge.

Masson, J. (2004), 'The legal context', in Fraser, S., Lewis, V., Ding, S., Kellett, M. and Robinson, C. (eds.) *Doing Research with Children and Young People*, London: Sage.

Mauthner, M., Birch, M., Jessop, J. and Miller, T. (eds.) (2002), *Ethics in Qualitative Research*, London: Sage.

McCosker, H., Barnard, A. and Gerber, R. (2001), 'Undertaking sensitive research: issues and strategies for meeting the safety needs of all participants', *Forum: Qualitative Social Research* 2,1: 22.

Mertens, D. and Ginsberg, P. (eds.) (2009), *The Handbook of Social Research Ethics*, California: Sage.

Milgram, S. (1963), 'Behavioral Study of Obedience', *Journal of Abnormal and Social Psychology*, 67 (4): 371–8.

Miller, T. and Bell, L. (2002), 'Consenting to what?: Issues of access, gate-keeping and "informed consent"', in Mauthner, M., Birch, M., Jessop, J. and Miller, T. (eds.) *Ethics in Qualitative Research*, London: Sage.

Montgomery, J. (2002), *Health Care Law*, Oxford: Oxford University Press.

Murphy, E. and Dingwall, M. (2007), 'Informed consent, anticipatory regulation and ethnographic practice', *Social Science and Medicine*, 65: 2223–34.

Neale, B. and Bishop, L. (2012a), 'The Timescapes archive: a stakeholder approach to archiving qualitative, longitudinal data', *Qualitative Research*, 12 (1): 53–65.

Neale, B. and Bishop, L. (2012b), 'The ethics of archiving and re-using qualitative longitudinal data: a stakeholder approach'. *Timescapes Methods Guides Series. Guide no 18.*

Oakley, A. (1981), 'Interviewing women: a contradiction in terms', in Roberts, H. (ed.) *Doing Feminist Research,* Boston: Routledge.

Oliver, P. (2003), *The Student's Guide to Research Ethics,* Maidenhead: Open University Press.

Orton-Johnson, K. (2010), 'Ethics in online research: evaluating the ESRC framework for research ethics categorisation of risk', *Sociological Research Online,* 15,4: 13.

Pauwels, L. (2008), 'Taking and Using: Ethical Issues of Photographs for Research Purposes', *Visual Communication Quarterly.* 15: 1–16.

Pels, P. (2008), 'What has anthropology learned from the anthropology of colonialism?', *Social Anthropology,* 16(3): 280–299.

Pink, S. (2007), *Doing Visual Ethnography Second Edition,* London: Sage.

Plummer, K (2001), *Documents of Life 2,* London: Sage.

Prosser, J. (2000), 'The moral maze of image ethics', in Simons H. and Usher R. (eds.) *Situated Ethics in Visual Research* (pp.116–132), London: Routledge Falmer.

Prosser, J. and Loxley, A. (2008), 'Introducing Visual Methods', NCRM Methodological Review. http://eprints.ncrm.ac.uk/420/

Punch, M. (1986), *The Politics and Ethics of Fieldwork,* California: Sage.

Realities Toolkit 6, *After the Ethical Approval Form: Ethical considerations of working in research teams.* http://www.socialsciences.manchester.ac.uk/morgancentre/realities/toolkits/research-team-ethics/index.html

Renold, E., Holland, S., Ross, N. and Hillman, A. (2008), '"Becoming participant": problematizing "informed consent" in participatory research with young people in care', *Qualitative Social Work,* 7,4: 427–447.

Research Ethics Guidebook http://www.ethicsguidebook.ac.uk/

The RESPECT Code of Practice (2004). http://www.respectproject.org/code/

Ritchie, J. and Lewis, J. (2003), *Qualitative Research Practice,* London: Sage.

Rodgers, J. (1999), 'Trying to get it right: undertaking research involving people with learning difficulties', *Disability and Society,* 14, 4: 421–433.

Rose, G. (2007), *Visual Methodologies: An Introduction to the Interpretation of Visual Materials,* London: Sage.

Rowe, M. (2007), 'Tripping over molehills: ethics and the ethnography of police work', *International Journal of Social Research Methodology*, 10, 1: 37–48.

Scratton, P. (2004), 'Speaking truth to power: experiencing critical research', in Smyth, M. and Williamson, E. (eds), *Researchers and Their Subjects: Ethics, Power, Knowledge and Consent*, Bristol: Policy Press.

Smyth, M. (2004), 'Using participative action research with war-affected populations: lessons from research in Northern Ireland and South Africa', in Smyth, M. and Williamson, E. (eds), *Researchers and Their Subjects: Ethics, Power, Knowledge and Consent*, Bristol: Policy Press.

Snee, H. (2008), *Web 2.0 As a Social Science Research Tool*. http://www.bl.uk/reshelp/bldept/socsci/socint/web2/report.html

Social Research Association (2001), *A Code of Practice for the Safety of Social Researchers*. http://www.the-sra.org.uk/guidelines.htm

Social Research Association (2003), Ethical Guidelines. http://www.the-sra.org.uk/guidelines.htm

Spicker, P. (2011) 'Ethical Covert Research', *Sociology*, 45: (1): 118–133.

Squire, C. (2008), *Approaches to Narrative Research*, NCRM Methodological Review Paper 008. http://eprints.ncrm.ac.uk/418/

Stanley, L. and Wise, S. (2010), 'The ESRC's Framework for Research Ethics: Fit for research purpose?', *Sociological Research Online*, 15, 4: 12. http://www.socresonline.org.uk/15/4/12.html

Sweetman, P (2009), 'Just anybody? Images, ethics and recognition', in Leino, R. (ed.) *Just Anybody* (pp. 7–9), Winchester: The Winchester Gallery, Winchester School of Art.

Tarleton, B., Williams, V., Palmer, N. and Gramlich, S. (2004), 'An equal relationship?: people with learning difficulties getting involved in research', in Smyth, M. and Williamson, E. (eds) *Researchers and Their Subjects: Ethics, Power, Knowledge and Consent*, Bristol: Policy Press.

Thelwall, M., and Sud, P. (2012), 'Webometric research with the Bing Search API 2.0', *Journal of Informetrics*, 6(1), 44–52.

Tilley, L. and Woodthorpe, K. (2011), 'Is it the end of anonymity as we know it? A critical examination of the ethical principle of anonymity in the context of 21st Century demands on the qualitative researcher', *Qualitative Research*, 11, 2: 197–212.

Tinker, A. and Coomber, V. (2004), *University Research Ethics Committees: Their Role, Remit and Conduct*, London: King's College.

Van den Eynden, Corti, L., Woolard, M., Bishop, L. and Horton, L. (2009), *Managing and Sharing Data*, Essex: UK Data Archive.

Van den Hoonard, W. (ed.) (2002), *Walking the Tightrope: Ethical Issues for Qualitative Researchers*, Toronto: University of Toronto Press.

Van Teijlingen, E. (2006), 'Reply to Robert Dingwall's Plenary "Confronting the anti-democrats: the unethical nature of ethical regulation in social science"' *Medical Sociology Online*, 1: 59–60.

Warwick, D. (1982), 'Tearoom trade: means and ends in research', in Bulmer, M. (ed.) *Social Research Ethics*, London: Macmillan Press.

Watts, J. (2008), 'Emotion, empathy and exit: reflections on doing ethnographic qualitative research on sensitive topics', *Medical Sociology Online*, 3, 2: 3–14.

Wiles, R., Heath, S., Crow, G. and Charles, V. (2005), *Informed Consent in Social Research: A Literature Review*. http://eprints.ncrm.ac.uk/85/

Wiles, R, Charles, V, Crow, G. and Heath S. (2006), 'Researching researchers: lessons for research ethics', *Qualitative Research*, 6,3: 283–299.

Wiles, R, Crow, G., Charles, V and Heath S. (2007), 'Informed consent and the research process: following rules or striking balances', *Sociological Research Online*, 12 (2). http://www.socresonline.org.uk/12/2/wiles.html

Wiles, R., Prosser, J., Bagnoli, A., Clark, A., Davies, K., Holland, S. and Renold, E. (2008), *Visual Ethics: Ethical Issues in Visual Research*. http://eprints.ncrm.ac.uk/421/

Wiles, R, Crow, G., Heath, S. and Charles, V. (2008), 'The Management of Confidentiality and Anonymity in Social Research', *International Journal of Social Research Methodology*, 11, 5: 417–428.

Wiles, R., Clark, A. and Prosser, J. (2011), 'Visual research ethics at the crossroads', in Margolis, E. and Pauwels, L. (eds.) *The Sage handbook of Visual Research Methods*, London: Sage.

Wiles, R., Coffey, A., Robison, J. and Heath, S. (2011), 'Anonymisation and visual images: issues of respect, "voice" and protection', *International Journal of Social Research Methodology*, DOI: 10.1080/13645579.2011.564423.

Wiles, R., Coffey, A., Robison, J. and Prosser, J. (2012), 'Ethical Regulation and Visual Methods: Making Visual Research Impossible or Developing Good Practice?', *Sociological Research Online*, 17 (1) 8. http://www.socresonline.org.uk/17/1/8.html

Williams, M., Dicks, B., Coffey, A. and Mason, B. (undated), 'Qualitative
data archiving and reuse: mapping the ethical terrain', Briefing Paper 2.
http://www.cf.ac.uk/socsi/hyper/QUADS/working_papers.html

Wright, S., Waters, R., Nicholls, V. and members of the Strategy for Living
Project (2004), 'Ethical considerations in service-user-led research:
strategies for living project', in Smyth, M. and Williamson, E. (eds)
Researchers and Their Subjects: Ethics, Power, Knowledge and Consent,
Bristol: Policy Press.

Xenitidou, M. and Gilbert, N. (2009), *Innovations in Social Science
Research Methods*, NCRM Working Paper. http://eprints.ncrm.
ac.uk/804/

Index

Printed in Great Britain
by Amazon

81180879R00070